AIR WAR
BOSNIA

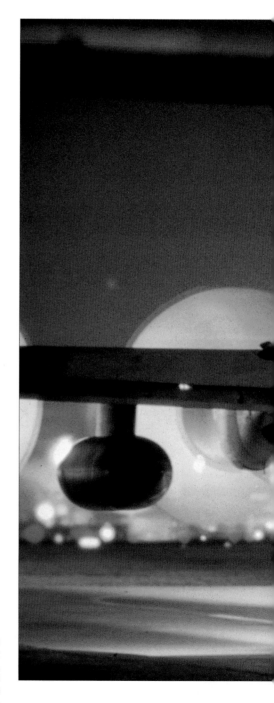

AIR WAR BOSNIA

UN and NATO Airpower

TIM RIPLEY

Motorbooks International
Publishers & Wholesalers ®

CREDITS

Over the past four years the author has received much assistance from UN and NATO personnel deployed to support operations in the former Yugoslavia. In particular I would like to thank the following:

Geneva: Ron Redman, UNHCR. **Sarajevo:** Lt Gen Sir Michael Rose, Lt Col Tim Spicer; Mr Andy Burridge, Thant Myint-U, BH Command; Col Jean-Claude Feve, French Air Force, Sarajevo Airport; Major Jorge de la Reta, Argentine Air Force; Capt Andy Lewis, 40 Regiment, RA. **Zagreb:** Lt Col Jan Reuterdahl, RSAF, Wing Cmdr RAF Chris Morffew, Mr Joe Warren, G3 Air Ops, Pleso; Capt Fred Hansen, NORMOVCON; Air Commodore John Houghton, RAF, NATO LO; LTC Don Watkins, USAF, Air Plans; Janel Schroeder, Paul Risley, Chris Gunness; Simo Vaatainen; Andrea Angeli, Mark Thompson, Paul Risley, UNPROFOR Division of Information; Lt Col Peter Crossman and Lt Col Walt Natynczyk, Canadian Army; Lt Col Jan-Dirk Van Merveldt and Lt Col Simon Barry, British Army; Rick Morgan, USN. **Split:** Maj David Falke and Lt Col Barry Hawgood, BRITFOR PIO; LTC Henk Giesbers, RNLAF, Air Ops Split; Maj Nick Caplin, Capt Dave Crisall, 664 Sqn AAC; 845 NAS; Det ALAT Split. **Mostar:** Lt Nicolas de san Roman Barrell, SPABAT. **Mt Igman:** Sgt Dave Cochrane and 5Pl, B Coy, 1 D&D. **Ploce:** Brig Robin Brims, Lt Col John Greenhalgh, AAC, Lt Col Roger Brunt, R ANGLIAN, Major Gerry Bartlett, PWRR, Major Mark Proffley, RLC, 24 Airmobile Brigade. Wing Cmdr Ian McKluskie, RAF, SHF. **Tuzla:** Col Goran Arlefak, Nordbat 2. **British Army:** Maj Pete Griffiths and Maj Pam Huggett, UKLF Media Production Cell; WOII Kevin Dodd and Capt James Gray, DDT. ECCM: Roger Vincent and Julian Gonzalez-Nunez. **Dutch MOD:** Martin Zijlstra. **AFSOUTH:** Maj Steve Headley, USAF; Lt Col Janice Witt, USAF, Francesco Veltri, Capt Jim Mitchell, USN; TSgt Keith Reid, USAF; LTC Dave Haas, USAF, AIRSOUTH. **5 ATAF:** Maj Gen Hal Hornburg, USAF; Brig Gen Dave Sawyer, USAF; Capt Ken Calise, USN; Capt Ed Fahy, USN; Brig Gen Serge Cocault and Brig Gen Gal Guevel, French Air Force; Gp Capt Richard Thomas, RAF; Col Herb Theis, Luftwaffe;. Special Thanks to Col G. Di Chio and Sgt Madonna. **Aviano:** Capt Tracy O'Grady-Walsh; Sgt Devon Fisher; A/C Dean C. Nash; LTC Gary West, 510th FS; Capt Wilbur Wright, 555th FS; Capt Shawn Mecham; Major Garcia De La Cruz and Maj Garcia Hernandez, SPAF. **Gehdi:** 142 Air Unit, Turkish Air Force. **Pisa:** 171 ARW (Deployed); LTC Dave Kramer, USAF and 91st ARS Det; LTC Dan Pegram USAF and 91st ARS Det. **Genoa:** LTC Dan Hale, Maj Marc Wrotny, 1st Lt Jeff Whiteman, 9th ARS Det. **Sigonella:** Lt Mark McCaffery, USN; Flt Lt Andy Maguire 101 Sqn, RAF; 19th ARW Det. **Gioia Del Colle:** Gp Capt Barry Titchen, RAF Det Co, Sqn Ldr Dave Allan, RAF, OC RIC. **USS America:** Lt Hal Pitman and JOC Paul Brown; Lt Cdr Steve Lowry and his PA Staff. **USS Theodore Roosevelt:** JOC (AW) G.L. Markfelder. **Bari:** HC-4 Det. **Op Sharp Guard:** RADM Elio Bolongaro, Italian Navy. **Ancona:** Sqn Ldr Stuart Vince; Flt Lt Mark White and crew of XV206; RAF Police Det for recovering my luggage from Sarajevo! **Operation Provide Promise:** Naples: Brig Gen James Jones, USMC. Rhein-Main: Col Larry Radov, LTC Harlan Ray, 37th AS and all his troops; All the reservists of the 38th AS. Rhein Main JIB: July 92, SSgt Robert Fortonberry: Oct 92, Capt Mike Rein: Mar 93, Major Cannon, SSgt Leonard Munson and SSgt Tom Mullighan: Jul 93, Capt Bob Jarvis and Airman Steve Ball: Mar 94, Capt Ray Cornellius: Jun 94 Capt Valerie Wilson and P/O Perkins: Jan 96, Maj Tom Dolney and his PA troops. **EUCOM:** Cdr Ron Morse. **US DoD:** Ken Carter. **CIOR:** Lt Cdr Scott Sanders, VAW-78 'Fighting Escargots'. Mark Cardwell, Canadian Army Reserve.

The Media Rat Pack: Paul Harris; Bob Morrison; Jeremy Flack; Alan Pizzy; Andy Clark and CBS TV Teams in Split and Sarajevo; Ray Canale; Leao Serva; Mike Ford; Nicolas Peucelle; Jim Cooper; Cliff Beale, Rupert Pengelley and David Miller IDR; Mike Gethings JDSM; Douglas Barrie, Forbes Mutch, Andrew Chuter and Alan Winn, Flight International; Bob Hall and Peter Felstead, JIR/Pointer; Paul Beaver, Jane's Sentinel; David Isby; Martin Streatley; David Morgan; Eric Hehs, Code One; All at David Farnell Photographic; Barry Wheeler, Air Pictorial; Roderick de Norman; Alan Burney, Aircraft Illustrated; World Air Power Journal, Jon Lake, Dave Donald, Tim Senior, Ron Hewson; Peter March and Brian Strickland, USAFB/RAFYB; Paul Jackson; Sarah Waddington, Peter Donaldson, John Osmond and Ian Parker, Defence Helicopter; Darko Hrastovec; John Holland. **RMAS Sandhurst:** Stuart Gordon. **And Finally:** Liz Campbell, HM Civil

This edition first published in 1996 by Motorbooks International, Publishers & Wholesalers, PO Box 1, 729 Prospect Avenue, Osceola, WI 54020, USA.

© 1996 Tim Ripley

Previously published by Airlife Publishing Ltd., Shrewsbury, England

Library of Congress Cataloging-in-Publication Data is available

ISBN 0-7603-0310-X

Printed in Hong Kong.

NOTES

1. Aircraft manufacturers' names. Over the course of the past four years a number of corporate mergers have occurred in the aviation industry leading to some changes in company names. As a point of style I have used the latest corporate identity for aircraft still in production, that is Lockheed Martin F-16C Fighting Falcon, but retained the name of the old company name for aircraft no longer in production, using the name in use at time of manufacture, that is Grumman F.14 Tomcat.

2. Squadron/unit names. Most Western air forces participating in NATO/UN air operations over Bosnia regularly rotated their units to forward bases in-theatre at two or three monthly intervals. As the campaign progressed it became increasingly common for unit identities to be merged to stand-up a squadron-sized detachment for a deployment. Often the responsibility fell on a squadron's home Wing or base to supply the necessary manpower and aircraft for a detachment. For that reason, it was very rare for a single squadron itself to provide all the manpower or aircraft for a detachment, so squadron/unit designations must be treated with some caution.

CONTENTS

FOREWORD

I first met Tim Ripley in the spring of 1995 in Vicenza, Italy, headquarters for NATO's Fifth Allied Tactical Air Force's Combined Air Operations Centre (CAOC), where he had come to interview me and others for a story on NATO air operations in support of the continuing operations in Bosnia. At the time, NATO was flying in Bosnia to uphold several United Nations Safety Council resolutions, such as the "No Fly Zone", and in support of the UN Protection Forces. For reasons best explained by others, military officers don't particularly relish interviews by unknown reporters, but in Tim Ripley I found a fresh, energetic approach to doing a piece on the contributions of airpower to a thorny and immensely complex military and political operation. While that was good news, even better was the fact that he told the story accurately and clearly, embellished only by wonderful photos of coalition aircraft and airmen who flew them.

Later that summer airpower proved pivotal in the most significant development of the tragic Bosnia conflict. Following the inhuman and totally senseless shelling of the Sarajevo market where 38 civilians were killed, the limits of tolerance were surpassed and, for the first time, NATO air power was able to be employed, unconstrained by UN restrictions. Within two weeks the future of Bosnia was reshaped and allowed diplomats to skilfully seize the opportunity to negotiate a peaceful solution. For the first time the use of air had brought about a significant political result without the need for a dedicated ground component to bring force to bear on Mother Earth. The air "campaign" was made to look relatively easy – it wasn't. It was superbly led by the air commander, Lt General Mike Ryan and his boss, Admiral Leighton Smith. It was closely co-ordinated with the ground commander in Sarajevo, Lt General Rupert Smith, a man of great wisdom and courage. I was privileged to exercise stewardship of the CAOC and was, therefore, the director of the day-to-day air operations with the tremendous help of a marvellous and highly talented international staff of motivated and tireless professionals. During the operation called Deliberate Force, NATO flew 3,515 missions, dropped 1,026 bombs on 338 aimpoints, all carefully selected by the commander to avoid collateral damage and loss of life. The aim was to encourage the Bosnian Serbs to find peace a better prospect than having their military capability systematically destroyed, and to do so without harm at the fringes of the operation. This was accomplished by good leadership, good planning and superb execution by some of the world's finest and most professional aviators. Every bomb was accounted for and not one aviator's life was lost, though one plane was shot down on the first day of the operation. For us in the CAOC, the operation ended only when the captured aircrew was released and returned to a heroic welcome in France.

So this book is about many things – Bosnia, freedom, and the right to live in peace. It is also about airplanes and courageous airmen who flew to make it so. As I write this I am in an airplane over Bosnia en route to a peaceful Sarajevo – just a year ago such a flight would but have been a dream.

Hal M. Homburg
Major General, USAF
June, 1996

Major General Hal Hornburg, USAF, as director of the 5th Allied Tactical Air Force's (5 ATAF) Combined Air Operations Centre (CAOC) at Dal Molin AB, Vicenza, Italy, had day to day control of all NATO air activity over the former Yugoslavia from November 1994 until the end of Operation Deny Flight on 20 December 1995. He then continued to serve in the same capacity as part of NATO's Implementation Force (IFOR). During the Gulf War he commanded the USAF's only McDonnell Douglas F-15E Strike Eagle Wing in Saudi Arabia.

INTRODUCTION

In the summer and autumn of 1992 I made two brief visits to the Bosnian capital to cover the United Nations High Commissioner for Refugees (UNHCR) airlift of humanitarian aid. On my first visit in July, the battle for Sarajevo was only three months old. In spite of the heavy house-to-house fighting of a kind not seen in Europe since World War Two, the UN soldiers in the city and allied airmen upheld an unbounded enthusiasm for their mission. Canada's Major General Lewis MacKenzie was still the commander of the UN's Sector Sarajevo and his charisma rubbed off on to his troops, who came from more than a dozen nations. They were going to make a difference, or so they thought. More than 14 air forces had contributed aircraft to make the airlift possible and room was at a premium at Zagreb's Pleso airport, in Croatia, which had become the operation's main aid loading hub.

Barely three months later I again flew into Sarajevo but the situation had been transformed. The optimism of the summer had been shattered by the shooting down of an Italian Alenia G222 airlifter 17 miles to the west of Sarajevo a month earlier. Only five countries – Britain, Canada, France, Germany and the United States – were prepared to put their aircraft at risk to kick start the airbridge back into life in the first week of October. Heavy rain, low cloud and bloody fighting around Sarajevo airport added to the gloom of those taking part in the aid mission. The failure of diplomatic efforts, culminating in the August London Peace Conference, to bring the war to an end created a mood of depression among UN personnel in Bosnia. With winter approaching there was a real threat of millions of people dying in those grim Balkan winter conditions. An inquiry into the loss of the Italian aircraft was unable to pin-point the owner of the heatseeking surface-to-air missile (SAM) that blasted it from the sky. However, UN officers and allied airmen concluded that, as the aircraft went down over Croat and Muslim held territory, the infamous Serbs were unlikely to be the culprits. The fact that the supposed beneficiaries of the international aid effort were turning on the UN was a big blow. Many of the UN and allied personnel wondered what kind of war they were getting involved in. One senior US commander at the time depressingly concluded that Sarajevo was a city 'full of people who want to kill each other'. Western air involvement would not be over by Christmas; this was going to be a long war.

The Bosnian War

Who fired the first shot in the Bosnian war will be a subject of intense debate for many years to come. As with all history in the Balkans, the truth is in the eye of the beholder. This is not really the place to study such a complicated subject. Up until the summer of 1991 the Republic of Bosnia–Herzegovina (BiH) was part of the Socialist Federal Republic of Yugoslavia. When conflict erupted Slovenia and Croatia demanded their independence from the Federal government in Belgrade, it was only a matter of months before the fighting spread to Bosnia.

At the time Bosnia had a mixed population with approximately half its people being of Muslim origin or religion. The remaining population was equally made up from people of Croat and Serb origin. There is considerable dispute as to why the war spread to Bosnia: the Muslims and many Croats claimed that the Serbs launched a bloody offensive to create a Greater Serbia, joined to the neighbouring Republic of Serbia; the Bosnian Serbs claimed they only wanted the right of self-determination on the same basis as the Croats and Muslims. What is clear, however, is that all the warring factions set about killing each other with great enthusiasm as soon the war got underway in April 1992.

Bosnia collapsed into the chaos of a brutal internal conflict, in which tens of thousands of people were to die and hundreds of thousands of others were made homeless over the next three years. The war was a conflict of shifting alliances that confused even the most learned students of the Balkan history. Initially the Muslim-led Army of Bosnia–Herzegovina (ABiH) was locked in battle with the Bosnian Serb Army (BSA), backed occasionally by elements of the old Yugoslav Federal Army (JNA). Croatians living in Bosnia formed their own militia, the Croatian Defence Council (HVO), which allied itself with the ABiH and were on occasions supported by regular troops from Croatia proper. By 1993 the Croats were at war with the Bosnians and some Muslims in north-west Bosnia changed sides to fight with the Serbs against the Sarajevo government. In early 1994 the Croats and Muslims had patched up their differences and again started joint operations against the Serbs. After the success of the Croatian offensives against the Serb-held Krajina and western Slavonia regions, the Croatian Army (HV) pushed into Bosnia to engage Bosnian-Serb troops.

International Response

As the violent conflict in the former Yugoslavia began to dominate international television reports in the spring and summer of 1992, world leaders started to come to terms with their response. None of the options looked good. Military intervention on the side of the predominately Muslim government of the Republic of Bosnia–Herzegovina, in Sarajevo, was not taken seriously in Western capitals. This would have entailed, in effect, declaring war with the Serbs and having to embark on a major land campaign to re-establish BiH authority over the territory of the Republic. There was no stomach for a Western-led war against the Serbs in the Balkans.

The UN had already launched a peace-keeping operation in Croatia, in March 1992, to police the ceasefire between newly independent Croatia and Serb forces. During the spring and summer of 1992, the United Nations Protection Force (UNPROFOR) was steadily being drawn into the conflict in neighbouring Bosnia, culminating in General MacKenzie's efforts to open Sarajevo airport for aid flights. A number of air forces then made aircraft available to the UNHCR to fly aid into the city. After the London Conference the UN mission was expanded to include escorting aid convoys throughout Bosnia. At the same time North Atlantic Treaty Organisation (NATO) members formally agreed to the alliance providing military assistance to the UN, at first only supplying personnel and equipment to set up UNPROFOR's Bosnia–Herzegovina Command (BHC) Headquarters. This decision opened the way for the use of airpower under alliance control to support UNPROFOR troops on the ground in Bosnia. NATO and the Western European Union (WEU), however, had been providing ships, maritime patrol aircraft and airborne early warning aircraft to monitor breaches of the UN arms embargo against the former Yugoslavia since July 1992, but these activities had no formal link to the UN forces in the country.

In 1992 the decisions made by Western leaders to limit military involvement in Bosnia, namely for humanitarian aid and so-called 'crisis management' measures to contain the conflict, set the agenda for UN and NATO air operations over the next three years. Western airpower would not be used for the benefit of one warring faction against the other, but to protect UN troops or dampen down major outbreaks of fighting. A sign in the BHC Headquarters in 1994 said 'Air should be used to move the road blocks on the road to peace – not destroy the goddam road'.

Tim Ripley
Lancaster
February 1996

Bosnia-Herzegovina, April 1995

SLOVENIA
HUNGARY
CROATIA
● Zagreb

SERB KARAJINA

CROAT
SERB

BiH
● *Bihac*

● Banja Luka

● Udbina

REPUBLIC OF

REPUBLIKA SERPSKA

SERB
CROAT

● Belgrade

SERB
CROAT

SERB

SERB
BiH

● *Tuzla*

BiH

SERBIA

BiH

○ Vitez

BiH
Srebrenica

○ Kisecjak

BiH
Zepa

● *Sarajevo*

● Gornji Vakuf

BiH
Gorazde

Adriatic Sea

SERB
CROAT

REPUBLIKA SERPSKA

HERZEG BOSNIA

BiH

● Split

BiH

● Jablinica

BiH

● Mostar

MONTENEGRO

● Ploce

CROAT
SERB

Key

SERB
B;H/CROAT — Confrontation line

Bihac □ UN safe area

– – – International border

SERB
CROAT

● Dubrovnik

Republika Serpska – Bosnian Serb   Herzeg-Bosnia – Bosnian Croat   BiH – Republic Bosnia-Herzegovina (Muslim)

NATO/UN Airbases in Former Republic Yugoslavia Theatre of Operations, Aug/Sept 1995

AUSTRIA
HUNGARY

● Aviano
Slovenia
Zagreb – Pleso

● Vicenza-Dal Molin
● Istrana

Croatia

● Ghedi
● Piacenza
● Verona-Villafranca

Bosnia-Herzegovina
● Tuzla

● Genoa

Gornji Vakuf
(helicopter only)

Kiseljak
(helicopter only)

Serbia

● Cervia

● Sarajevo

Ligurian Sea

● Pisa

● Ancona-Falconara

Split-Divulji Barracks ●

Ploce Dockyard Camp ●

Adriatic

ITALY

Sea

Montenegro

Camp Able Sentry – Skopji

SARDINIA

● Bari

ALBANIA

Fyro-Macedonia

● Naples-Capodinichino

● Brindisi

● Elmas

● Gioia del Colle

Tyrrhenian Sea

GREECE

Mediterranean Sea

● Palermo

Ionian Sea

SICILY
● Sigonella

CHAPTER 1
OPENING THE AIRBRIDGE TO SARAJEVO, JULY–SEPTEMBER 1992

Sarajevo airport lies to the west of the city, nestling in a large valley. In 1992 to the west of the runway was the Bosnian-held village of Butmir. The Bosnian-held suburb of Dobrinja, with its concrete apartment blocks, was to the east of the airport terminal complex. To the north, right underneath the glide path, was the Serb stronghold of Ilidza. Serb-held high ground was to the south and east of the runway. Dominating the airport is Mount Igman, rising high above Butmir, which is the 'vital ground' in the Sarajevo region and would it be fought over with great intensity by both the Bosnian Serb Army (BSA) and the predominately Muslin Army of Bosnia–Herzegovina (ABiH) for the next three years. The airport would become one of the most important pieces of real estate in Bosnia and the focus of UN and NATO air operations.

In May 1992 Sarajevo airport was firmly in the hands of the Yugoslav Federal armed forces (JNA), who were supporting the BSA troops fighting ABiH forces around the city. UNPROFOR had originally planned to base the headquarters for its Croatia peace-keeping operation in Sarajevo but the heavy fighting, which began a month earlier, had compelled the international force to flee to the safety of the Serbian capital Belgrade. In June UNPROFOR negotiated a deal with the BSA and ABiH leaderships to take over control of the airport for a humanitarian airlift of food and medicine to begin.

This original agreement was to become the basis for the operation of the airport over the next three and half years. It was often the only justification for the UN to stay in the city at all, given the unwillingness of the warring factions to respect any peace agreement or ceasefire.

Mitterand arrives

Thanks largely to the determination of Canada's Major General Lewis MacKenzie, who had been appointed commander of UNPROFOR's newly created 'Sector Sarajevo' a few days earlier, the airport received its first flight on 28 June in the shape of French President Francois Mitterand. His dramatic arrival by French *Armée de l'Air* Aérospatiale SA-332 Super Puma helicopter caught General MacKenzie by surprise, but the media attention surrounding the visit seemed to deter the warring factions from interfering with the UN operation to open the airlift – at least for the present.

A French *Armée de l'Air* Lockheed Martin C-130H Hercules landed during the following evening to kick start the airlift. Over the next three days more French Hercules and C.160 Transall airlifters arrived carrying the personnel and equipment needed to get Sarajevo airport's battered facilities back in operation. A guard force of 125 French Marine infantrymen were also flown in to provide security until a battalion of Canadian mechanised infantry could make the journey overland from Croatia.

On 3 July the UNHCR airlift officially started, although aid flights had been landing occasionally over the past couple of days. With the Canadian and French troops in place, along with the French *Armée de l'Air* airport operation's team handling the unloading, air traffic control and other services, the pace of activity started to speed up. At first it was under ten aircraft per day but as more nations offered to provide aircraft the schedule was expanded to take around 20 flights per day. Croatian airports at Pleso, near the capital Zagreb, and Split, on the Adriatic, became the main hubs for the airlift effort. The USAF, however, operated out of Rhein–Main AB, near Frankfurt in Germany.

Aircraft would shuttle into Sarajevo with pallets of aid, which would be off-loaded in under 15 minutes by forklifts operated from the joint French unloading and Norwegian movement control team, then fly out to re-load before making the hop back into Sarajevo. There was only one small unloading area available at Sarajevo with room for only three large aircraft at the most, so the flow of aircraft into the airport had to be tightly controlled to prevent backlogs. No pilot wanted to spend more time than absolutely necessary on the ground so it was not to difficult to enforce air traffic discipline on the multi-national force of aircraft assembled for the operation. The Air Operations Cell (AOC) at UNHCR Headquarters in Geneva co-ordinated the efforts of 14 air forces taking part in the airlift providing flight slots and other information.

At the height of the summer airlift aircraft arrived from the air forces of Belgium, Britain, Canada, Denmark, France, Germany, Greece, Italy, Norway, Saudi Arabia, Spain, Sweden, Turkey and the United States of America. Aircraft from UNPROFOR's own fleet of chartered airlifters also regularly made the dangerous journey to Sarajevo. 'There were more aircraft stacked up in Zagreb waiting to fly in than we could handle,' declared General MacKenzie.

Taking fire

The original agreement with the warring parties to open the airport called for no hostile acts to be made against aid aircraft using the airport. Yet, in the chaotic situation prevailing in Sarajevo during the summer of 1992, it was only a matter of time before airlifters started taking fire. A couple of aircraft picked up bullets and a British Royal Air Force C-130 was 'locked-on' to by a radar guided anti-aircraft system. On occasions UNPROFOR closed down the airport as fighting raged under the flight path, with aircraft being waved off when on final approach.

The airlift continued to struggle on for two months, clocking up more than 1,000 sorties into the city, but the 'threat level' became unacceptable on 3 September when an *Aeronautica Militare Italiana* Alenia G222 was targeted by a shoulder-fired, heat seeking, surface-to-air missile (SAM) some 17 miles from Sarajevo airport. The aircraft lacked self-defence systems to decoy the missile which hit an engine, blowing off one wing. The four crew were killed. A United States Marine Corps combat search and rescue (CSAR) package of two Sikorsky CH-53E Sea Stallions and two Bell AH-1W Super Cobras were fired upon by Croat troops as they approached the crash site.

Immediately the UNHCR shut down the airlift operation and it would again be over a month before aid would be flown into Sarajevo. Most nations withdrew their poorly protected airlifters and the burden of the operation would fall on five NATO air forces, which had airlifters equipped with self defence systems, when the airlift re-opened in October.

An *Aeronautica Militare Italiana* Alenia G222 transport, similar to this example shown at Split in the summer of 1995, was lost to hostile fire on 3 September 1992. After this tragic incident the Italians largely limited their air involvement to flights in the relative safety of Split and Zagreb that supported Italian elements of the European Community Monitoring Mission, the European Union administration in Mostar and a variety of humanitarian aid projects. In September 1995, Italian airmen joined their NATO colleagues in Operation Deliberate Force air strikes. *(Tim Ripley)*

This panorama graphically illustrates how exposed the unloading area at Sarajevo airport was to hostile fire. French Army anti-sniper teams used to monitor suspected firing points and retaliate to any 'in-coming' shots, but flight crews of aircraft were virtually defenceless in their cockpits. *(Tim Ripley)*

In the summer of 1992 Sarajevo airport's terminal building still boasted glass windows. Over the years the windows would be replaced by wooden boards and earth ramps. By comparing the photos in this chapter with those in later ones it is possible to follow the gradual fortification of the airport complex by the UN. *(Tim Ripley)*

The seige of Sarajevo 1992 as seen from a French SPOT satellite. *(MATRA Space)*

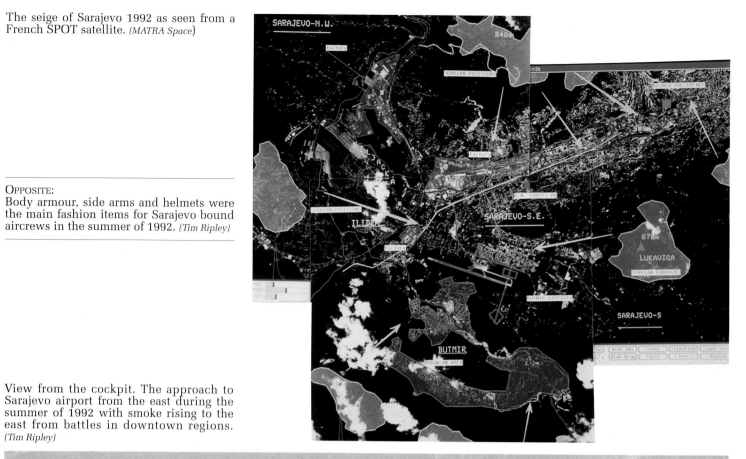

OPPOSITE:
Body armour, side arms and helmets were the main fashion items for Sarajevo bound aircrews in the summer of 1992. *(Tim Ripley)*

View from the cockpit. The approach to Sarajevo airport from the east during the summer of 1992 with smoke rising to the east from battles in downtown regions. *(Tim Ripley)*

Large Antonov An-12 airlifters were
chartered by the United Nations Protection
Force (UNPROFOR) in summer of 1992 to
move heavy cargoes around its mission
area in the former Yugoslavia and they
flew many sorties into the Bosnian capital
before being replaced by the jet powered
Ilyushin Il-76s *(Tim Ripley)*

French *Armée de l'Air* unloading teams soon perfected the techniques needed to empty airlifters of their cargo pallets in as short a time as possible. It was rare for aircraft to be on the ground for more than 25 minutes. Engines were kept running to allow for rapid take-offs in case of emergency. *(Tim Ripley)*

The USAF 37th Airlift Squadron (AS), based at Rhein-Main, flew the first American aircraft to land at Sarajevo, but they were soon augmented by aircraft of the 317th Airlift Wing (AW) and reserve components equipped with airlifter defense systems (ADS) to protect them from heat-seeking SAMs. This is a 317th (AW) aircraft. *(Tim Ripley)*

French *Armée de l'Air* cargo handling teams at Sarajevo could unload a C-130/C.160 in under 10 minutes. Many of their forklifts were donated by British, Canadian and US air forces. *(Tim Ripley)*

The German *Luftwaffe* was quick to get involved in the UNHCR operation and stuck with it through to the end. The *Luftwaffe's* three transport Wings (Lufttransportgeschwader) 61, 62 and 63 all shared this burden over three and-a-half years, flying C.160D Transalls. *(Tim Ripley)*

The *Force Aerienne Belge*'s 20 Squadron joined the UNHCR airlift at Zagreb for the first two months of the mission before being withdrawn home. *(Tim Ripley)*

Aeronautica Militare Italiana Dassault Falcon 50, of 31 Stormo, made the dangerous journey into Sarajevo during July 1992 to enable European Union diplomats to attempt to broker a series of futile ceasefires. *(Tim Ripley)*

17

CHAPTER 2
MAYBE AIRLINES: THE SARAJEVO AIRBRIDGE, OCTOBER 1992 – JANUARY 1996

'Maybe Airlines' was the unofficial name for the fleet of international aircraft that flew UNHCR humanitarian aid into Sarajevo. 'Maybe the plane comes, maybe not, maybe it lands, maybe not, maybe it gets shot at, may be not' was its motto, coined by the UN peacekeepers, aid workers diplomats and journalists who relied on the airbridge to take them into the heart of the Bosnian conflict. The name was no slur on the airmen who flew the airbridge but a comment on the precarious nature of trying to keep an airport open in the middle of a battlefield.

With the re-opening of the airbridge to Sarajevo in October 1992, the operation of the city's airport settled into a routine of sorts. No one could, however, rely on the airport being open. The weather around the airport was terrible, with fog hanging over the valleys around Sarajevo and low cloud drifting down from Mount Igman. Every couple of weeks aircraft would be shot at and the airport closed down for varying periods of time. Eventually the airport would re-open and business resume. Users had to be prepared for the unexpected.

Airbridge

Building the airbridge each day was the job of the UNHCR Air Operations Cell (AOC) at the organisation's Geneva headquarters. A team of seconded military officers worked with veteran aid workers to build the daily flight schedule that brought many types of humanitarian aid to Sarajevo. Even on days when Sarajevo airport was closed, the AOC still had to put together the schedule just in case the threat level dropped or the weather cleared.

Getting aircraft in the air was the responsibility of the multi-national Joint Air Operations Cell (JAOC) at Ancona-Falconara Airport, in Italy, and UNPROFOR's G3 Air Operations at Pleso Camp, at Zagreb. The JAOC contained representatives of the British Royal Air Force, Royal Canadian Air Force, French *Armée de l'Air*, German *Luftwaffe* and United States Air Force. In early 1993 this nerve centre relocated to Ancona from Zagreb after most of the participating nations decided to move away from the Croatian capital. It was not until early 1995 that all the air forces involved in the operation based their aircraft at Ancona. The French had been operating from Split and the USAF was based at Rhein–Main AB, in Germany. Each air force usually provided one or two aircraft per day to fly missions into Sarajevo. On occasions other air forces or aid organisations sent aircraft to join the operation for short periods, such as the Royal Swedish Air Force and the British Overseas Development Agency, who would be merged into the JAOC set-up.

Flying out of Pleso was the UNPROFOR fleet of white painted chartered aircraft. There were regularly tasked to fly into Sarajevo with personnel or equipment for the UN garrison in the city and occasionally aid shipments. UNPROFOR made good use of Ilyushin Il-76 heavy lift, multi-purpose Antonov An-26 transports and Yakovlev Yak-40 VIP aircraft. They were flown by former Soviet Air Force pilots, who learnt their trade landing at Kabul airport in Afghanistan.

On a good day up to 30 slots into Sarajevo were available for in-bound flights. Not surprisingly there were no overnight parking facilities. Places on aircraft were available on a first come, first served basis. There were, however, strict rules governing who could fly on the aircraft because of the terms of the original agreement with the warring factions over the use of Sarajevo airport.

Every passenger and cargo was searched to ensure that no unauthorised weapons or contraband were carried. At Sarajevo airport Serb and Bosnian liaison officers were present during unloadings to make certain no unauthorised cargoes were carried. On the one hand this prevented either side claiming the UN was helping the other. But, on the other hand, it gave the warring factions the ability to interrupt the airlift when they felt like it. The Serbs would occasionally 'refuse to guarantee the safety' of aid aircraft after NATO airstrikes against them, while the Bosnian Government refused to permit aid to Sarajevo in February 1993 because of Western refusal to bomb the Serbs attacking the Muslim-held town of Srebrenica. In early 1994 Bosnian objections to allow Serb liaison officers into Tuzla airport prevented the UNHCR extending their aid airlift to the northern Bosnian city. 'I'd rather let my people starve than let a single Serb into Tuzla,' commented the Bosnian commander in Tuzla.

In August 1993, a major effort was put into increasing the number of evacuations of wounded civilians from Sarajevo who needed urgent medical attention outside the wartorn city. The British lead the way with their Operation Irma evacuation of a crippled Bosnian schoolgirl.

Except for the tragic loss of the Italian aircraft in September 1992 no aircraft were lost to hostile fire during operations into Sarajevo, although a chartered Il-76 crash-landed in January 1995 in strong wind. Its ruined carcass remains at the end of the Sarajevo runway as a land mark for careless pilots. There were some 270 'security incidents' involving the airlift until it officially came to an end on 9 January 1996, of which 50 are thought to have involved aircraft actually taking hits. None of these hits were catastrophic and the aircraft were all able to make it to a friendly airport safely.

At the conclusion of the airlift some 12,951 sorties had been flown into Sarajevo airport, making it the longest running airlift in history, easily surpassing the famous Berlin airlift. A total of 160,677 metric tons of aid and 15,850 metric tons of medical supplies was flown into Sarajevo. Often the airlift was the only way to get aid into the city after fighting or political problems closed convoy routes. 'The airlift was Sarajevo's lifeline and constant reminder to the thousands of brave residents of the city that they were not forgotten,' said UN High Commissioner for Refugees, Sadako Ogata. 'Without a doubt, the airlift saved tens of thousands of people and kept the city alive through three winters of war.

Always on alert. The flight crew of a Lockheed C-141B Starlifter keep watch for hostile fire during the final descent into Sarajevo in June 1994. By now the cockpits of all airlifters flying into Sarajevo had Kevlar armour fitted. *(Tim Ripley)*

Joint Task Force Provide Promise badge, created for members of the US armed forces who were participating in delivering humanitarian aid to the former Yugoslavia. It was not only worn by aircrews at Rhein-Main AB, Germany, but by personnel at the JTF Headquarters in Naples, Italy, and on the ground in Bosnia with the UN. *(Tim Ripley)*

NORMOVCON badge. This small team of Norwegian Movement Control personnel played a key role in the UNHCR airbridge by co-ordinating passengers and cargo at Sarajevo, Pleso and Split airports. They were also responsible for most of the 'Maybe Airlines' T-shirts and badges that aircrews collected. Their famous 'Maybe Airlines' passport stamp at Sarajevo airport was even reportedly personally confiscated by UN chief Yasushi Akashi, who did not see the joke! *(Tim Ripley)*

Sarajevo airport tower was manned by French *Armée de l'Air* air traffic controllers throughout the airbridge operation. It was protected by bullet proof glass that replaced shattered windows but a sign inside declared 'You are now standing in one of the most dangerous places on earth!' *(Tim Ripley)*

20

The Royal Swedish Air Force, of F7 Squadron, re-joined the UNHCR operation in 1993 for a number of months after its Lockheed Martin C-130E/H Hercules were equipped with self-defence systems. They flew a number of the casualty evacuation missions to take out civilians from Sarajevo after the February 1994 market massacre. *(USAF/JCC(D))*

USAF Lockheed C-141B Starlifters, of the 347th Airlift Wing (AW), joined the airlift operation in May 1994 for almost three months until an aircraft picked up 22 bullets on 20 July. *(Tim Ripley)*

Armoured fire engines were provided by the French *Armée de l'Air* and proved invaluable at Sarajevo airport. *(Tim Ripley)*

UNPROFOR used charted Ilyushin Il-76s to fly in supplies to its garrison in Sarajevo, and they were also tasked to fly in humanitarian aid. *(Tim Ripley)*

View from the cockpit. Aircraft used very steep approaches to reduce their vulnerability to small arms fire when taking-off or landing at Sarajevo. The Serb-held suburb of Ilidza was right under the flight path and it was very easy for disgruntled Serbs to take out their frustration on the UNHCR aircraft. Bosnian militia men in Butmir and Dobrinja were also know to take pot-shots at the UNHCR aircraft in attempts to close down the airlift and hence put up the price of food on the black market. *(Tim Ripley)*

The threat from heat-seeking hand-held surface-to-air missiles (SAMs) was taken very seriously after the events of 3 September 1992, so UNHCR aircraft and UNPROFOR helicopters were fitted with defence systems that launched flares to decoy SAMs. French Army Aviation (ALAT) Aérospatiale SA-330B Pumas for the ALAT Detachment, based at Split from late 1992, were fitted with the MATRA Saphir system. *(MATRA)*

The most dangerous job in Sarajevo. A French airman guides an Armée de l'Air C.160F Transall to its unloading spot at the city's airport. *(Tim Ripley)*

The United Nations High Commissioner for Refugees (UNHCR) badge sported on Sarajevo-bound aircraft. *(Tim Ripley)*

The vulnerability of aircraft approaching Sarajevo airport is apparent by this view from the downtown area. Mount Igman, a major battlezone, is towering above the airport. *(Tim Ripley)*

Chartered East European Ilyushin Il-76s proved popular with both UNPROFOR and aid agencies such as the UNHCR and Britain's Overseas Development Agency. These two Il-76s were visiting Sarajevo in November 1994. *(Tim Ripley)*

Senior UN military commanders, international diplomats and aid workers made use of UNPROFOR's two Yakovlev Yak-40 VIP aircraft. *(Tim Ripley)*

CHAPTER 3
FEEDING THE ENCLAVES, SPRING 1993

To starving Bosnians in besieged towns along the Drina River in eastern Bosnia, they were the 'planes from God'. Cut off for months by marauding bands of Serb troops, the enclaves of Srebrenica, Zepa, Gorazde and a number of smaller villages, were on the verge of collapse. Food was short, electricity non-existent, disease and malnutrition was rampant. Serb forces refused to allow aid convoys or UN peace-keepers through into the enclaves.

Newly elected President Bill Clinton ordered the USAF to start air dropping supplies to the enclaves to stave off a humanitarian disaster. UNPROFOR commanders and aid workers in Bosnia were initially very sceptical about American claims that they could deliver the aid in the quantities required to the enclaves, but as the operation got underway this attitude changed.

In February 1993 the USAF 435th Airlift Wing at Rhein–Main AB, near Frankfurt, was give the task of conducting the airdrop phase of Operation Provide Promise, as the US contribution of UN operations in the former Yugoslavia was code named. The burden of the operation fell on the 37th Airlift Squadron (AS) with their 19 veteran Lockheed Martin C-130E Hercules. This was soon boosted by the arrival of reinforcements from stateside active duty units, along with Air Force Reserve and Air National Guard elements.

Due to the threat from Bosnian Serb fighters and anti-aircraft systems, all the airdrop missions were to be flown at night at medium altitudes, which made it very challenging for the aircrews to get their cargoes into the small drop zones around the enclaves. This meant that mass drops could not be used because there was only room in the sky above the small drop zones for a single aircraft at a time, so the air drop formations had to approach the enclaves in line astern formation with aircraft separated by strict timing. In the darkness of Bosnia there would little room for error if the airdrop aircraft strayed from their course and collided in mid air. If the cargoes missed the drop zone there was a danger that innocent civilians away from the drop zones could be hit by the heavy metal bases of the food pallets. For that reason drop zones outside towns were selected and the locations were radioed to aid workers or UN Military Observers in the enclaves so that collection of the cargoes could be arranged. Starting on 28 February, the Americans sent nightly formations over eastern Bosnia to drop their aid cargoes. At first it was only three aircraft, then six and then nine at a time, as the USAF crews gained experience and confidence.

General Morillon calls

While the USAF was getting the airdrop operation into high gear at Rhein–Main, a crisis was unfolding in the enclave of Srebrenica where the UNPROFOR commander, French Lieutenant General Philippe Morillon, was being held hostage by the local Bosnian commander. US Special Force officers in Srebrenica and General Morillon kept in contact with the Joint Task Force Provide Promise Headquarters in Naples by satellite radio. They provided details of drop zones around the town to the USAF crews at Rhein–Main and the flow of aid to the enclave increased. General Morillon arranged a ceasefire to allow wounded to be evacuated by UNPROFOR helicopters. British Royal Navy Westland Sea King HC.4s and French Army Aviation (ALAT) Aérospatiale SA-330B Pumas flew to the UN-held Tuzla airbase in northern Bosnia from Divulji Barracks at Split on the Adriatic coast in preparation for their mission into the enclave. In mid-March the French and British helicopters tried to make it into Srebrenica but the Serbs fired on the landing zone.

It would be a month before the air evacuation effort could get fully underway after UN Canadian troops moved into the enclave to set up the first so-called 'safe area'. During March as the airdrop operation gathered momentum, the French and German governments sent aircraft to Rhein–Main to help in the aid effort. Three German and one or two French C.160s Transalls were to be based at Rhein–Main for over a year, flying daily missions as part of the US led airdrop formations. Over the summer of 1993 and into the autumn, six USAF C-130s, along with a French and German aircraft, would make night forays into Bosnian air space delivering aid to enclaves throughout Bosnia that were unable to receive regular aid convoys. Considerable effort was put into improving the packaging of aid pallets to reduce the danger to people on the ground in Bosnia. USAF and US Army cargo riggers developed the so-called Tri-Wall Aerial Distribution System (TRIAD), which was basically a cardboard box containing US military MRE ration packs. The box was pushed out of the back of a C-130 and broke up in flight creating a 'cluster food bomb' effect below. In August 1993 this system was used to drop food to the Muslim-held eastern sector of Mostar city. Journalists in the city reported the sky was 'raining food'.

Delta Squadron

As winter approached in late 1993, the United States government decided to significantly step-up its contribution to Operation Provide Promise. A second composite C-130 Hercules squadron, dubbed the 38th Airlift Squadron (Provisional)(AS(P)) or Delta Squadron, was formed at Rhein–Main to allow nine aircraft per night to drop aid to the enclaves and four aircraft to fly into Sarajevo every day. This brought the size of the Hercules force at Rhein–Main to some 44 aircraft drawn from the 37th AS, 38th AS(P), augmented by active duty aircraft from the 317th Airlift Wing and reserve component units.

By the early summer of 1994, the need for air dropping to enclaves was significantly reduced thanks to a general decrease in levels of fighting throughout Bosnia. The end of the Croat–Muslim war in early 1994 saw the opening up a number of enclaves, such as Maglai, that had been besieged by Croat and Serb troops. In eastern Bosnia aid convoys were able to reach the enclaves on a regular basis after the UN increased its troop presence in Gorazde, Srebrenica and Zepa. Delta Squadron's C-130s had all returned home by June after flying the last of its airdrop missions on 10 June. The final airdrop mission was flown by the 37th AS, along with a German C.160D to Bihac on 19 August but the mission attracted heavy Serb anti-aircraft artillery fire and future air drops to the enclave were permanently put on hold. By then some 2,828 airdrop sorties had been flown by the French, German and US aircraft to deliver 18,002 metric tonnes of aid. Lieutenant General Sir Michael Rose, UN commander in Bosnia during 1994, said 'Everyone laughed at [airdropping aid] when it first came. It has kept many thousands of people alive in the enclaves through two winters. It has been highly successful.'

Lieutenant Colonel Harlan Ray, USAF, as commander of the 37th Airlift Squadron (AS) flew the first mission over eastern Bosnia of Operation Provide Promise dropping leaflets on 27 February 1993, which warned about the dangers of being underneath aid pallets. He was a veteran of numerous missions to Sarajevo since the previous July. *(Tim Ripley)*

German *Luftwaffe* C.160D Transalls were based at the Rhein-Main AB for over a year from 15 March 1993 flying around 400 air drop missions over besieged enclaves in Bosnia. Lufttransportgeschwader 61 and 63 took turns to provide a three aircraft detachment at the US base near Frankfurt. *(Tim Ripley)*

Rosi

Each pallet had its own parachute which slowed the pallet down and kept it on course for the small drop zones. (USAF/JCC(D)) (Top Facing: Tim Ripley)

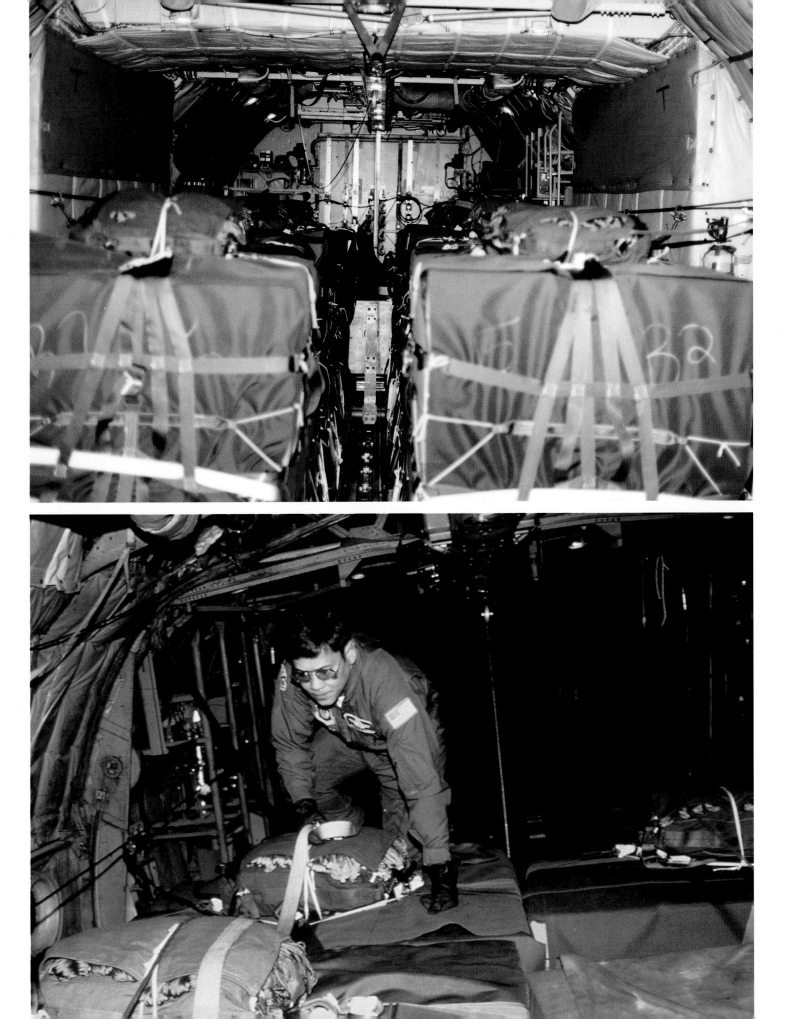

Aid pallets leave a USAF Lockheed Martin C-130 Hercules over eastern Bosnia, as filmed with a night-vision device. All lights had to extinguished inside the airdrop aircraft to protect them from ground surveillance. *(USAF/JCC(D))*

To reduced the risk of casualties from the heavy pallets, the USAF and US Army cargo riggers at Rhein-Main came up with the Tri-Wall Aerial Distribution System (TRIAD), which was basically a cardboard box that broke apart in flight scattering the drop zone with small military MRE ration packs. It was a 'food cluster bomb.' *(USAF/JCC(D))*

American leaflets dropped over eastern Bosnia in 1993 warning about the dangers of being under a 500kg aid pallet when it impacted with the ground! They were written in Serbo-Croat and Cyrillic script.

ABOVE:
Night-time launch from Rhein-Main. Up to a dozen aircraft at a time, including spares to cover for breakdowns, were prepared for each night-time air drop sortie over eastern Bosnia. *(USAF/JCC(D))*

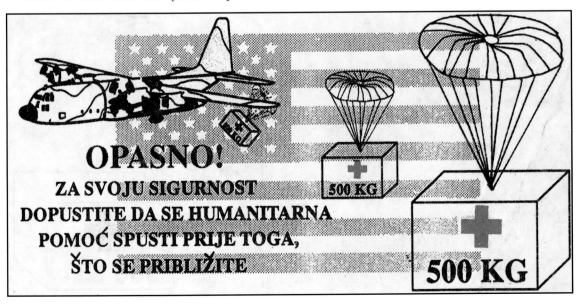

33

Senior officer from US European Command visited Rhein-Main in C-21A Learjet 35A to co-ordinate Operation Provide Promise. *(Tim Ripley)*

Mission accomplished. An empty Lockheed Martin C-130 Hercules taxies into its parking space at Rhein-Main. There was always a great deal of apprehension as the aircraft returned from the missions and ground crew would wait for them back on the runway, in much the same way as ground crews at US bomber bases in World War Two. This mission involved bombing the target with food! *(USAF/JCC(D))*

The badge of Lufttransportgeschwader 63, which took part in airdrops over Bosnia from March 1993. *(Tim Ripley)*

Delta Squadron Badge. Worn by crews of the 38th Airlift Squadron (Provisional), which was formed in January 1994 when the airdrop operation at Rhein-Main was expanded by an influx of USAF Reserve and Air National Guard personnel and aircraft. The additional assets allowed an effective doubling of the airdrop effort in the depths of the winter months of early 1994. *(Tim Ripley)*

The badge of Lufttransportgeschwader 61, which took part in airdrops over Bosnia from March 1993. *(Tim Ripley)*

The 37th Airlift Squadron (AS) provided the core of the Operation Provide Promise effort throughout 1992 and into 1994 when Rhein-Main started to be run down. The other badge is of a visiting German unit. *(Tim Ripley)*

Casualties from Srebrenica were evacuated to Tuzla by British Royal Navy Westland HC.4 Sea King, of 845 Squadron, and French Army Aviation (ALAT) Aérospatiale SA330B Puma helicopters, of the Det ALAT Split. This was the first major operation for the white-painted British and French helicopters, which arrived at Split on the Adriatic coast in late 1992 to support UNPROFOR. *(ECPA/SIPRA)*

The Germans arrive. Amid much publicity the German *Luftwaffe* deployed three C.160Ds to Rhein-Main on 15 March 1993. *(Tim Ripley)*

US Navy Grumman F-14A Tomcats and McDonnell Douglas F/A-18C Hornets, flying from the USS *John F Kennedy* and then the USS *Theodore Roosevelt* in the Adriatic, were always in the air during the air drops ready to intervene should the slow-moving transports come under attack from Serb fighters or surface-to-air missile (SAM) units. *(USAF/JCC(D))*

US Navy Attack Squadron (VA) 36 on the USS *Theodore Roosevelt* were also ready to provide close air support if a major rescue operation had to be mounted in the face of opposition. *(Tim Ripley)*

Northrop Grumman E-2C Hawkeyes of US Navy Carrier Airborne Early Warning Squadron (VAW) 124, from the USS *Theodore Roosevelt*, and VAW-126, from the USS *John F Kennedy*, provided airborne early warning support for the air drop aircraft while they were over eastern Bosnia. *(Tim Ripley)*

CHAPTER 4
DENY FLIGHT BEGINS, SPRING 1993

During early Serb offensives in Croatia and Bosnia, ground attack aircraft and helicopter gunships of the Federal Yugoslav armed forces (JNA) flew daily missions to neutralise pockets of resistance. When Serb republics were declared in Bosnia and the Krajina region of Croatia in the spring of 1992, the JNA transferred a number of air units to the two new state's armed forces. Business continued as usual with both air forces combining to carry out important joint operations to attack pockets of Croat and Muslim resistance in northern and western Bosnia during the following summer.

The indiscriminate nature of many of these air strikes, involving civilian casualties forced action from the UN Security Council, who ordered a ban on all flights over Bosnia in October 1992, except those authorised by UNPROFOR. NATO's Airborne Early Warning Force (NAEWF) Boeing E-3A AWACS, along with French *Armée de l'Air* E-3Fs and British Royal Air Force E-3Ds, began conducting surveillance of Bosnian airspace on 16 October to monitor compliance with the no-fly zone. The AWACS had been on patrol in the region since July supporting NATO and WEU ships in the Adriatic that were monitoring the UN arms embargo against the former Yugoslavia.

Not surprisingly, the warring factions in Bosnia showed total disregard for the ban and continued to fly their military aircraft. The UN ban was not going to get in the way of their war plans. The use of air support by Serb forces during the attack on Srebrenica in March 1993 finally snapped the patience of Western powers, who pushed the UN to start enforcing the no-fly zone.

On 12 April 1993 the first NATO combat air patrols (CAPs) of Operation Deny Flight were launched over Bosnia to drive military aircraft from the skies. NATO's 5th Allied Tactical Air Force (5 ATAF) was given the mission of conducting the operation. It set up a Combined Air Operation Centre (CAOC) at its headquarters at Dal Molin AB, near Vicenza, Italy, to co-ordinate all allied air activity over the Balkans.

British, Dutch, French, Turkish and US fighters, based in Italy or on aircraft carriers in the Adriatic, flew around the clock CAPs over Bosnia looking for unauthorised air activity. AWACS aircraft flying over the Adriatic or Hungary detected the violators and passed on the information to the CAOC, who would then task the fighters to investigate.

CAP stations

Air refuelling was essential to make the operation work. The fighters only carried limited fuel and they needed to top up their tanks over the Adriatic before crossing the Croatian coast to go 'feet dry' over Bosnia. They would then spend around an hour on CAP, flying around Bosnia looking for trade, before returning to the tanker track over the Adriatic to take on more fuel. A further hour on CAP would follow before they then headed for home. During the first months of Deny Flight, a pair of fighters each maintained two CAP stations over Bosnia for 24 hours a day. A constant stream of fighters was always coming or going to ensure

fully fuelled and armed NATO fighters were over Bosnia. The presence of heavily armed fighters overhead seemed to have the desired effect on the Bosnian Serb air force, who kept their ground attack aircraft on the ground at Banja Luka air base. However, the Krajina Serb air force kept flying at Udbina in western Croatia but they did not venture into Bosnian airspace.

ROE

NATO fighter pilots still saw a lot of helicopter and light aircraft activity as all the warring factions tried to fly in arms and move people around Bosnia. Due to the political sensitivities of these flights the UN and NATO decided that Deny Flight fighters could only engage and shoot down any aircraft that were actually carrying out combat operations – dropping bombs, firing guns or rockets. There was a big fear that a helicopter carrying wounded civilians would be shot down by NATO fighters, creating very bad media headlines. The US government was also afraid that NATO would shoot down a Bosnian or Croat helicopter. In spite of the no fly zone being imposed to stop the Serbs using their combat aircraft, the Bosnians and Croats were also regularly breaching the ban. Liaison officers were exchanged between NATO and UNPROFOR to allow speedy exchange of flight scheduling information concerning UN flights. To avoid mistakes, very tight rules of engagement (ROE) were put in place by 5 ATAF. Thus, before an alliance fighter pilot could intercept or engage a no-fly zone violator, a three or four star general NATO officer at the CAOC had to agree. Crucially there was no 'duel key' with the UN concerning air engagements. If the ROE requirements were met then NATO aircraft could go into action against violators without the permission of UN ground commanders and this in fact happened in February 1994 when Krajina Serb strike aircraft ventured into Bosnia to attack Bosnian arms factories near Novi Travnik. Four USAF Lockheed Martin F-16C Fighting Falcons intercepted the six Serb jets and shot four of them down. It took only three minutes for the CAOC to give permission for the fighters to engage their targets.

That was a near perfect engagement. The difficult thing was finding a good target. For the first 11 months of Deny Flight the Bosnian and Krajina Serb air forces stayed well away from NATO fighters. In the first months of Deny Flight, NATO pursued an aggressive policy of intercepting helicopters and forcing them to land or leave the no-fly zone. NATO fighters were authorised to drop down into the valleys of Bosnia to buzz the helicopters and this seemed to have the desired effect, but after the fighters had to leave to the area to refuel the helicopters simply started up their engines and carried on with their activity. This became a very frustrating time for NATO fighter pilots and eventually it was decided to stop wasting time and fuel chasing helicopters around Bosnia. It became every NATO fighter pilots dream to come across a flight of bomb-laden Serb SOKO Geleb aircraft. NATO achieved its mission of putting the Bosnian and Krajina Serb air forces out of business with only one air-to-air engagement.

Theatre Air Base (TAB) shelters were home at Aviano to USAF McDonnell Douglas F-15C Eagles of the 53rd Fighter Squadron, which deployed to Italy from their home base in Germany. *(USAF/JCC(D))*

Opposite Below and Above:
French *Armée de l'Air* Dassault Mirage 2000C, of 5e Escadre de Chasse, operated from Cervia in support of Operation Deny Flight. One of these aircraft was lost on the first night of the mission during an in-flight refuelling accident. *(USAF/JCC(D))*

Controllers aboard the NATO Airborne Early Warning Force (NAEWF). British and French AWACS aircraft monitored all activity in the former Yugoslavia, dispatching Deny Flight fighters to investigate possible violators of the UN no-fly zone. *(USAF/JCC(D))*

NATO fighters maintained around the clock combat air patrols over Bosnia, requiring a constant flow of aircraft into the area of responsibility, to ensure constant coverage by the fighter patrols. *(USAF/JCC(D))*

Lockheed Martin F-16A/B Fighting Falcons of the Royal Netherlands Air Force's 315th Squadron were among the first wave of NATO aircraft to deploy to Villafranca AB, Italy, for Operation Deny Flight in April 1993. Six F-16(R)s of 306th Squadron were also sent to Italy to provide NATO with a photographic reconnaissance capability. *(USAF/JCC(D))*

Turkish Top Gun. The *Turk Hava Kuvvetleri* was one of the best Turkish units. The 142 Filo (squadron) was equipped with home-produced Lockheed Martin F-16C Fighting Falcon fighters to join Operation Deny Flight. *(Tim Ripley)*

British Royal Air Force Panavia Tornado F.3 fighters, of No 11 Squadron, took part in Operation Deny Flight from Gioia del Colle AB, in southern Italy, from 19 April onwards. *(Tim Ripley)*

Turkish Lockheed Martin F-16C Fighting Falcons joined Operation Deny Flight late on 20 April after the Greek government refused overflight rights to their NATO 'allies'. *(Tim Ripley)*

Carrier airpower. US Navy F/A-18c of the US Marine Corps patrolled Bosnia from the USS *Theodore Roosevelt* for the first six months of Deny Flight. *(USAF/JCC(D))*

CHAPTER 5
SAFE HAVENS: NATO BEGINS CLOSE AIR SUPPORT FOR UN, SUMMER 1993

NATO's mission over Bosnia was to undergo a major change during the summer of 1993 after the dramatic events of the spring around Srebrenica and collapse of the Vance–Owen Peace Plan, which was seen as the last hope to end the war without major bloodshed.

The US-sponsored Joint Action Plan (JAP) was developed in an attempt to contain the effects of the Bosnian war. It was formally adopted by the UN on 4 June, opening the way for NATO to be given the mission of providing close air support (CAS) for UNPROFOR troops operating in the so-called 'safe areas'. This was not the green light for widespread airstrikes to turn the tide of war against the Serbs but only the bombing of hostile forces actually engaged in carrying out direct attacks on UNPROFOR troops. By placing UN troops in the six safe areas – Bihac, Gorazde, Sarajevo, Srebrenica, Tuzla and Zepa – it was felt that they would deter attacks on them. If CAS aircraft were overhead ready to intervene, it was hoped the warring factions would think twice about targeting UNPROFOR troops.

NATO strike aircraft started to flow into Italian bases during July 1993 and by 22 July the alliance declared it was ready to provide CAS for UNPROFOR. Operation Deny Flight was expanded to include the around the clock patrols of fully bombed-up CAS aircraft over Bosnia, ready to respond within minutes to calls for help from UN troops under attack.

Most UNPROFOR battalions were provided with Tactical Air Control Parties (TACP), which had the necessary communications and target-locating equipment to guide NATO strike aircraft to their targets. NATO aircraft regularly trained with the TACPs establishing communications with them during their missions over Bosnia and practising the procedures for engaging targets. USAF Lockheed Martin EC-130E Airborne Battlefield Command and Control Centre (ABCCC) aircraft flew daily missions over the Adriatic to be on station to relay CAS requests from TACPs, to in-bound strike aircraft, the 5th Allied Tactical Air Force's (5 ATAF) Combined Air Operations Centre (CAOC) at Vicenza, in Italy, and the UN Air Operations Control Centre (AOCC) at Kislejak, just outside Sarajevo.

While the links between NATO pilots and UN forces on the ground worked well, there was considerable uncertainty about the high-level decisions over the political authorisation of CAS. At this point the UN Secretary-General Boutros Boutros Ghali, was insisting that he had to personally authorise any air strikes in Bosnia. This required UNPROFOR commanders to contact him in New York before NATO airpower could be called into action. It was the infamous 'dual key' arrangement.

Mount Igman

July 1993 saw the intensity of fighting dramatically increase in Bosnia with a Serb offensive against Mount Igman to the south of Sarajevo. Croat and Muslim forces were locked in bloody battles in central Bosnia and around Mostar. UNPROFOR troops found themselves stuck in the middle of this conflict with little means of influencing events. French troops came under Serb tank fire in Sarajevo and Spanish troops based at Jablanica were shelled by Croats.

NATO started to use its new capability to provide what was termed as 'air presence' for UN troops under threat, with strike aircraft flying over the incident area to deter the warring factions from causing trouble.

Warring faction commanders had no way of knowing that it could be hours before the UN Secretary-General could be contacted to give his approval for the aircraft to engage their targets. The presence of a pair of fully armed Fairchild A-10A Warthogs was usually intimidating enough to resolve the problem.

Serb successes on Mount Igman, however, provided the potential to escalate further because their advance was threatening to close the noose around the Bosnian government's only route into Sarajevo via their tunnel under the airport runway. The US Government began to press for widespread air strikes against the Serbs to reverse their gains on Mount Igman and so began the first 'Sarajevo air strike ultimatum crisis'. On 9 August NATO issued an ultimatum to the Serbs to pull back. NATO aircraft made their presence felt over Sarajevo and within days the Serbs backed down and a French UN force took control of a demilitarised zone on Mount Igman.

Calling in CAS

Towards the end of August UNPROFOR increasingly began to rely on air support to provide its troops with muscle if things looked like getting nasty. USAF A-10As buzzed Mostar on 27 August to deter the Croats and Serbs from shelling the city while a Spanish UN convoy was trapped in the Muslim eastern sector. Just over a week later US Navy A-6E Intruders were called in to help British troops when their base at Vitez came under Croat fire. In both cases the NATO air presence had the desired effect: the UN troops were left alone with no ordnance having to be put on target.

Two months later a UN Nordic battalion patrol was trapped in the middle of a three-sided battle between Croats, Serbs and Muslims, near the northern Bosnian town of Dastansko. The Swedish commander asked for NATO air support and within minutes, Warthogs were buzzing the valley creating plenty of noise. Three UN soldiers held hostage were released unharmed and the Nordic troops could return to base.

As winter approached Bosnia remained in the grip of bitter fighting. International peace efforts had yet to come to anything, while UNPROFOR troops and NATO airpower seemed to be having a marginal effect on the situation.

Deadly feline. A British Royal Air Force SEPECAT Jaguar GR. Mk.1A on close air support alert at Gioia del Colle, Italy, ready to scramble to support UN troops under attack. *(Tim Ripley)*

Aircrew humour at Aviano AB, Italy. It seems the Fairchild A-10A Warthog pilots of the 510th Fighter Squadron (FS) AKA 'The Buzzards' were not impressed by the international diplomacy designed to bring the Bosnian war to an end. *(Tim Ripley)*

OPPOSITE:
The remains of a USAF Lockheed Martin F-16C Fighting Falcon, of the 23rd Fighter Squadron (FS), being fished out of the Adriatic in August 1993 after it crashed in a non-combat incident. *(USAF/JCC(D))*

Lockheed S-3B Vikings, of US Navy Antisubmarine Squadron (VS) 11, operated in the overland surveillance mode from the USS *America*, looking for strike targets in Bosnia, thanks to Project Aladdin which modified their radar APS-137 inverse synthetic aperture system. *(Tim Ripley)*

USS *America* brought with her 22 McDonnell Douglas F/A-18C Hornets from Navy Strike Fighter Squadrons 82 and 86 when she took over Adriatic duty from the USS *Theodore Roosevelt* in late August 1993. *(Tim Ripley)*

Vital communications links between NATO airpower and UNPROFOR ground troops were maintained by USAF Lockheed Martin EC-130E Airborne Battlefield Command and Control Centre (ABCCC) aircraft of the 7th Airborne Command and Control Squadron. The aircraft's rear cargo hold was filled with hi-tech computer consuls and communications links to allow combat controllers on board to speak to almost every 'player' in the Balkan theatre of operations. (USAF/JCC(D))

Carrier Air Wing 1 badge. The Air Wing controlled all the aircraft embarked on the USS *America*. *(Tim Ripley)*

Fairchild A-10A Warthogs, of the 510th Fighter Squadron (FS), were soon in demand by UNPROFOR commanders to over fly hot spots and intimidate the warring factions into letting the peacekeepers get on with their job of delivering humanitarian aid. *(USAF/JCC(D))*

McDonnell Douglas F/A-18D Hornets of Marine All-Weather Fighter Attack Squadron (VMFA(AW)) 533 flew multi-role missions over Bosnia – combat air patrol, close air support and airborne forward air control – to take advantage of the two-seat Hornet's impressive day and night capabilities. *(USAF/JCC(D))*

USAF Fairchild A-10A Warthogs, of the 510th Fighter Squadron, were dual roled as close air support and airborne forward air controller. In the later role they flew with white phosphorous rockets to allow them to mark targets for other NATO strike aircraft. *(USAF/JCC(D))*

CHAPTER 6
SUPPORT MISSIONS

While NATO's fighters and strike aircraft were at the cutting edge of the alliance airpower, a major force of support aircraft was deployed to keep them in the air.

Tankers

Fundamental to the 5th Allied Tactical Air Force (5 ATAF) concept of operations was air-to-air refuelling (AAR). Almost every aircraft that flew over Bosnia made use of AAR in some form because of the lack of forward bases for NATO aircraft within the former Yugoslavia.

Refuelling tracks were established over the Adriatic Sea, where tankers circled waiting for NATO fighters to come out from their patrols over Bosnia to take on fuel. Fortunately the weather over the Adriatic was usually far better than that in-land making taking-on fuel relatively easy. There were some moments of excitement, including a French *Armée de l'Air* Dassault Mirage 2000C ingesting a Boeing KC-135 refuelling drogue into its engine during a night-time refuelling. Fortunately the pilot was rescued after ejecting over the Adriatic.

A major problem for 5 ATAF planners was the incompatability between the USAF's boom and the European/US Navy probe-drogue refuelling systems. This reduced the flexibility of the NATO tanker fleet, a factor which was made worse because the KC-135, the main American and French tanker, could only be converted to one or the other system on the ground. The USAF McDonnell Douglas KC-10A Extender, which boasted both systems, was only made available to 5 ATAF on two occasions – June 1995 and later in the year for Operation Deliberate Force. The arrival of the aircraft in-theatre was a major force-multiplier.

AWACS

Aerial surveillance of Bosnia was the job of the NATO Airborne Early Warning Force (NAEWF), assisted by the British and French Air Forces. Every allied aircraft that entered Bosnian airspace was tracked by the Boeing E-3 Sentry Airborne Warning and Control System (AWACS) to ensure they did not fly into each other and could be kept aware of any hostile threats.

Using the callsign 'Magic', the NAEWF E-3As, British E-3Ds and French E-3Fs were on station 24 hours a day in orbits over the Adriatic and Hungary, using their powerful radars to look for violations of the no-fly zone. They were then able to vector NATO fighters to investigate. US Navy Northrop Grumman E-2C Hawkeye AWACS aircraft also helped out on this effort when American carriers were supporting Operation Deny Flight.

The E-2s and E-3s also acted as a communications relay between NATO fighters and the 5 ATAF Combined Air Operations Centre (CAOC) at Vicenza, passing back authority to investigate and engage no-fly zone violators. Warnings about hostile radar activity from electronic intelligence (ELINT) gathering aircraft was also passed to NATO fighters via the AWACS.

Britain, France, Germany and the United States also shared the job of maintaining an orbit of ELINT aircraft over the Adriatic to detect hostile surface-to-air missile (SAM) radar activity throughout the former Yugoslavia.

British Royal Air Force BAe Nimrod R.Mk.2s, French *Armée de l'Air* C.160 Gabriels and Douglas DC-8 Sarigues, German *Marineflieger* Dassault-Breguet 'Peace Peek' Atlantics, US Navy Lockheed Martin EP-3E Areis II, US Air Force Boeing RC-135 Rivet Joints and Lockheed Martin U-2Rs were always on station and played a key role in protecting NATO aircraft from SAMs.

Embargo

NATO and the WEU warships were sent to the Adriatic in July to monitor the UN arms embargo against the former Yugoslavia but within months they had begun to enforce the embargo, along with economic sanctions against Serbia and Montenegro. These efforts were merged into Operation Sharp Guard in June 1993. To support the embargo operations, maritime patrol aircraft (MPA) were deployed to Italy to patrol the Adriatic and Ionian Seas looking for embargo busting shipping. US Navy Lockheed Martin P-3Cs Orions and *Aviazione per la Marine Militare* Dassault-Breguet Atlantics home based at Sigonella on Sicily, were regularly assisted by RAF Nimrods, Canadian CP-140 Auroras, Spanish, Dutch and Portuguese Orions. French and German Atlantics, also helped out from the Italian Atlantic base at Elmas on Sardinia.

From the summer of 1993 the MPA flew armed with anti-submarine torpedoes because of the threat from Serbian Navy submarines to the Sharp Guard forces. To provide protection from Serb surface forces the *Aeronautica Militare Italiana* placed Tornados armed with Kormoran anti-ship missiles on alert at Gioia del Colle and they were scrambled in May 1994 when Serb ships tried to ram British and Dutch ships arresting a Serbian-bound tanker in the Adriatic. With the arrival of the Tornados overhead the three Serb ships headed for home and the oil tanker was impounded.

CSAR

The prospect of having to bale out over Bosnia, either as a result of hostile fire or mechanical problems, was not something that filled any NATO pilot with any confidence, so combat search and rescue (CSAR) assets were kept on constant alert in Italy or on ships in the Adriatic. USAF Special Operations Forces Sikorsky MH-53J Pave Low III helicopters and their associated Lockheed Martin HC-130 Combat Shadow III tankers were based at Brindisi in southern Italy along with French *Armée de l'Air* Aérospatiale SA330B Pumas. The land-based assets took turns on alert with US Marine Corps units on assault ships or US Navy SEALs based on aircraft carriers. This CSAR effort was overseen by 5 ATAF's Combined Rescue Co-ordination Centre at Vicenza.

Movers

Moving senior commanders and time critical cargoes quickly around the Balkan theatre of operations was an important consideration for NATO and UNPROFOR. The Spanish Air Force provided 5 ATAF with a CASA C.212 aircraft with which to do this task and UNPROFOR had its own fleet of Yakovlev Yak-40 for the same job. Usually senior officers and diplomats could call upon the services of their respective air forces to provide VIP transport around the theatre. Flying into Sarajevo, however, was a different matter and most security conscious VIPs would jump ship, at Split or Ancona, to fly into the city on board a 'Maybe Airlines' C-130 or C.160. Not only did the UNHCR-assigned aircraft boast better self-defence systems but they also had more experienced crews and did not attract unusual attention on the exposed tarmac at Sarajevo.

Two Yakovlev Yak-40s were chartered by
UNPROFOR to fly its senior commanders
and diplomats around the former
Yugoslavia. During many missions to
Sarajevo they came under sniper fire.
(Tim Ripley)

Royal Danish Air Force Gulfstream III VIP
jets, of 721 Squadron, were regular visitors
to the former Yugoslavia carrying Danish
military chiefs and European Union
diplomats. *(Tim Ripley)*

Aeronautica Militare Italiana Panavia Tornado, of 36 Stormo, were scrambled from Gioia del Colle in May 1994 to provide top cover for NATO ships in the Adriatic after the Serb Navy came out from port to challenge the UN embargo.

The boom operator of a Boeing KC-135 Stratotanker at work during a Deny Flight mission over the Adriatic. It was the job of the 'boom' to steer the refuelling boom into position. *(USAF/JCC(D))*

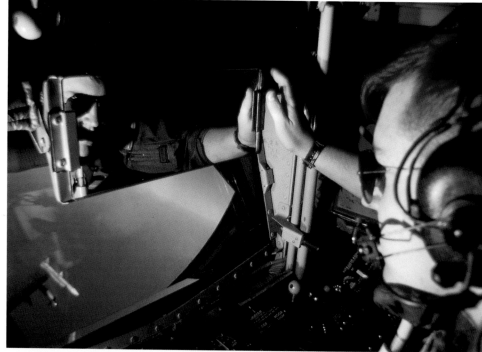

A busy Boeing KC-135 Stratotanker cockpit during a Deny Flight refuelling mission. NATO tanker crews had to weave their way through Italian air traffic control zones to reach their refuelling tracks over the Adriatic. *(USAF/JCC(D))*

The view from the cockpit. A Lockheed Martin EC-130E Airborne Battlefield Command and Control Centre (ABCCC) aircraft pulls up behind a Boeing KC-135 Stratotanker to take on fuel over the Adriatic. *(USAF/JCC(D))*

German *Marineflieger* Westland Lynx Mk 88 Lynx helicopters, of the 3 Staffel./Marinefliegergeschwader 3, were used to land boarding parties on ships in the Adriatic suspected of attempting to breach the UN arms and trade embargoes of the former Yugoslavia. *(NATO/AFSOUTH)*

OPPOSITE:
Italian Agusta-Bell 212AS helicopters, of the *Aviazione per la Marine Militare*, were regularly in action landing boarding parties of the San Marco Marine Battalion onto ships in the Adriatic suspected of attempting to breach the UN arms and trade embargoes of the former Yugoslavia. *(Tim Ripley)*

Tanker art work at Pisa, Italy. This indentified the tenants as being the 43rd Air Refuelling Group's (ARG) 91st Air Refuelling Squadron (ARS).

Sigonella-based Sikorsky SH-53E Sea Stallions, of the US Navy's Helicopter Combat Support Squadron (HC) 4, provided key logistic support for US Navy and allied ships operating in the Adriatic. It was a regular occurrence for two of the giant heavy lift helicopters to be forward based at Bari to provided support for carrier battlegroups. *(Tim Ripley)*

Tanker humour at Sigonella. NKAWTG is tanker talk for 'Nobody Kicks Ass Without Tanker Gas'. The RAF Mildenhall-based 100th Air Refuelling Wing (ARW) and its 351st Air Refuelling Squadron (ARS) provided administrative support for all stateside based detachments to Italy and France in support of Operation Deny Flight. *(Tim Ripley)*

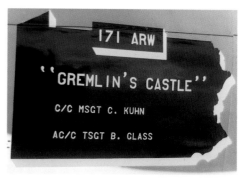

Tanker artwork on a Boeing KC-135E Stratotanker, of the 171st Air Refuelling Wing, (ARW) Pennsylvania Air National Guard at Pisa, Italy. *(Tim Ripley)*

Royal Navy aircraft carriers operating in the Adriatic often received visits from UN tasked Westland Sea King HC.4s based at Split in Croatia. *(UKLF Media Production Cell)*

USMC Boeing CH-46E 'Frogs' and Bell UH-1N 'Hueys', of Marine Helicopter Squadron, Medium (HMH) 264, were key components of Marine Expeditionary Unit (Special Operations Capable) (MEU(SOC)) aviation elements. The composite squadron was part of the 26th MEU(SOC) in May 1993. *(Tim Ripley)*

British Royal Air Force VC10 K. Mk.2s, of No 101 Squadron, deployed to Sigonella in April 1993 to support the British Deny Flight contingent but were replaced two months later by No 216 Squadron Lockheed Tristar K. Mk.1s. *(Tim Ripley)*

Close circuit television was used to monitor air refuellings on board British Royal Air Force VC10 K. Mk. 2 tankers. *(Tim Ripley)*

British Royal Air Force VC10 C. Mk.1 transports, of No 10 Squadron, made weekly 'milk runs' carrying supplies and personnel to RAF and Royal Navy detachments in Italy and the British Army at Split in Croatia. *(Tim Ripley)*

US Navy Lockheed Martin P-3C Orion maritime patrol squadrons spent six-month detachments at Sigonella to support the NATO embargo operations in the Adriatic. *(Tim Ripley)*

This Lockheed Martin VP-3A Orion served as the 'Admiral's Barge' or VIP aircraft for the US Navy Admiral serving as NATO's Allied Force Southern European (AFSOUTH) commander. It was home based at Sigonella. *(Tim Ripley)*

A rare photograph of a US Navy Lockheed Martin P-3C Orion, of Patrol Squadron (VP) 26, armed with AGM-65 Maverick guided missiles during a test firing mission from Sigonella, in the January 1994. These weapons were employed on Orions at Sigonella especially for operations in the Adriatic. *(US Navy/ JO3 Joe Clark)*

CHAPTER 7
BLUE SWORD IN ACTION: NATO AIR STRIKES IN 1994

In January 1994 the UN mission in the former Yugoslavia was at a low ebb with its commanders disillusioned by the unwieldy 'dual key' arrangements for the control of NATO air strikes and the warring factions regularly treating its soldiers with contempt. The situation was transformed with the arrival in Sarajevo on 24 January of British Lieutenant General Sir Michael Rose as commander of the UN's Bosnia-Herzegovina Command (BHC). He set about re-invigorating the UN effort in Bosnia and was quickly confronted with a major challenge when a mortar shell landed in a Sarajevo market on 5 February killing 68 Bosnian civilians. It has never been discovered who fired the mortar; it could have been a Serb terror attack or Bosnian Army attempt to generate good television coverage in America. Senior UN commanders thought both sides were possible culprits.

NATO leaders in Brussels then decided to issue an ultimatum to the Serbs ordering them to remove all their heavy weapons 20km from Sarajevo by 20 February or face massive air strikes. At the same time General Rose struck a deal with the Serbs giving them the chance to place their artillery and tanks in so called 'weapons collection points' within the exclusion zone under UN supervision.

In Italy, the 5th Allied Tactical Air Force (5 ATAF) stepped up the tempo of its operations to prepare for the air strikes if they were ordered. Photographic reconnaissance aircraft criss-crossed Sarajevo looking for Serb gun positions, tanks, ammunition dumps, barracks and command posts. NATO was preparing a massive strike to knock-out the Serb forces besieging the city. USAF McDonnell Douglas F-15E Strike Eagles and other reinforcements were sent to Italy to give 5 ATAF a strong laser guided bomb delivery capability and in-theatre NATO strike aircraft also started to sport precision guided munitions.

This brinkmanship played dividends and the Bosnian Serb leadership soon got the message that they had better back down. The arrival of Russian UN troops significantly reduced tension and the Serbs pulled back their artillery. While Sarajevo may now have been quiet, this did not mean that fighting had subsided in the rest of the country and on numerous occasions over the coming months NATO jets were called in to calm the situation when UNPROFOR troops came under fire from the warring factions.

Gorazade

A major battle developed in the eastern enclave of Gorazde during the first week of April as Serb troops pushed back Bosnian defenders from the heights above the town. A small team of unarmed UN Military Observers (UNMOs) in the town had been reinforced, on General Rose's orders, by a squad of British SAS Commandos, trained as forward air controllers (FACs). On 10 April they came under fire while patrolling the frontline and requested NATO close air support (CAS) or 'Blue Sword' as it was code-named by UNPROFOR. By now the responsibility to authorise CAS had been delegated to the UN Secretary-General's Special Representative in the former Yugoslavia, Mr Yasushi Akashi. He rapidly agreed with General Rose that action was needed to protect the SAS soldiers. A USAF EC-130E Airborne Battlefield Command and Control Centre (ABCCC) aircraft organised the request for CAS, handing over a pair of USAF Lockheed Martin F-16C Fighting Falcons to the FACs who directed them to their targets. The Serbs held back briefly but the following day they renewed their onslaught. An EC-130E maintained a constant flow of aircraft over the enclave to deter further attacks but more air strikes were called for and two US Marine Corps McDonnell Douglas F/A-18As Hornets attacked.

The situation remained tense and NATO aircraft continued to patrol the town. Terrible weather prevented photo reconnaissance aircraft getting good pictures of what was going on. This problem was made worst on 15 April when a French *Aéronautique Navale*

Dassault-Breguet Etendard IVP was hit by a SA-7 heat-seeking surface to air missile (SAM). It managed to safely land back on its carrier. A British Royal Navy BAe Sea Harrier FRS.1 did not survive a similar hit the following day and the pilot soon found himself a guest of the Bosnians. Bad weather prevented USAF Fairchild A-10A Warthogs finding Serb guns firing on the SAS later in the day. General Rose now ordered the SAS out of the town and French Army Aviation (ALAT) Aérospatiale SA330B Pumas dodged across Serb held territory to bring out the British soldiers and downed pilot. NATO leaders now lost patience with the Serbs and ordered a heavy weapon exclusion zone to be set up or widespread air strikes would be launched against the Serbs surrounding Gorazde. This again led to the Serbs backing down and a 500-strong contingent of UN troops were allowed into Gorazde to police the new zone.

Sarajevo summer

Around Sarajevo the UN and the warring factions were locked into a series of confrontations that were escalating out of control. The Bosnians and Serbs played cat and mouse with the UN to ensure the other was blamed for the breakdown of the precarious peace established by General Rose around the city. Bosnian troops fired mortars at the UN-controlled airport in the hope that the Serbs would get the blame for closing down the UNHCR airlift. The Serbs in turn tried to sneak their artillery and tanks from the weapons control points and engage the Bosnians. When the Serbs removed two armoured vehicles and anti-aircraft gun on 5 August, General Rose ordered a punitive airstrike after they refused to return the weapons. A US Air National Guard A-10A then pumped 600 rounds of 30mm cannon fire in an abandoned Serb tank in a demonstration of NATO's firepower. A similar air strike occurred on 22 September, after a French UN armoured vehicle was struck by Serb anti-tank fire, with a RAF SEPECAT Jaguar hitting a Serb tank with a 1,000lb bomb. The Serbs promptly retaliated by closing Sarajevo airport until 7 October.

Udbina

The Bihac enclave in north western Bosnia now became the main flash-point after the Bosnia Army's 5th Corps staged a major offensive out of the town. Bosnian Serb forces engaged in a large counter-attack with the co-operation of Krajina Serb forces across the border in Croatia. During November, Krajina Serb air force strike aircraft from Udbina staged hit-and-run raids across the border to bomb Bihac. NATO fighters were vectored to intercept but they could not catch the Serb planes before they could get back across the border, which was only a couple of minutes flying time away. The UN quickly agreed to NATO plans to strike at Udbina to deter further Serb air strikes, and 5 ATAF put in train plans to destroy Udbina's runways and air defences. On 21 November a 30 aircraft strong NATO strike package took off to attack Udbina and used laser guided bombs, Maverick missiles, cluster bombs and iron bombs to inflict heavy damage on Udbina's facilities. The attacks were very accurate and the Serb aircraft based there played no further part in the crisis for many months to come.

Over Bosnia, tension remained high with a Royal Navy Sea Harrier almost being hit by a Serb SAM on 22 November. In response, 5 ATAF began to protect its photographic reconnaissance patrols with heavy suppression of enemy air defence (SEAD) forces. Strike Eagles armed with laser guided bombs, USAF General Dynamics EF-111A Raven jammers, USMC Grumman EA-6B Prowlers and Hornets armed with AGM-88 High Speed Anti-Radiation Missiles (HARM) were sent over Bosnia waiting for Serb SAM activity. On 23 November the Serbs fell into the trap and switched on their SAM radars near Bihac. The NATO package pounced, firing three HARMs in return. Later in the day

NATO returned to bomb a SAM site that remained active and fired three more HARMs at other missile batteries.

The Serbs thought NATO was about to launch its much heralded widespread air strikes and started to retaliate against UNPROFOR troops in Bosnia. UNMOs were tied to the runway at Banja Luka to deter NATO air attacks and 300 UN troops taken hostage in weapons collection points around Sarajevo. Around Bihac the Serbs continue to press their attack, culminating in General Rose threatening to bomb their tanks firing into the town on 25 November. A 30-strong aircraft strike package centred around Hornets and Strike Eagles was launched from Aviano AB, in Italy, to put the tanks out of action. The firing ceased before the aircraft could attack and General Rose called off the strike.

UNPROFOR now decided to de-escalate the crisis and requested NATO keep its aircraft out of Bosnian airspace until the Serbs were in a less aggressive mood. The Serbs took the hint and started to release the UN hostages and allow aid convoys to move through their territory to the enclaves. With the winter snow arriving the warring factions had largely stopped fighting and they readily agreed to a ceasefire until the spring. With still no movement on reaching a political solution to the war, 5 ATAF and UNPROFOR were not looking forward to what 1995 would bring.

French *Armée de l'Air* Dassault Mirage 2000K-2 strike aircraft, of 4e Escadre de Chasse (EC), played an important role in the NATO air strike on Udbina in November 1994. *(Tim Ripley)*

Capt Bob (now Major) "Wilbur" Wright, USAF, engaged and shot down three Serb aircraft over Bosnia on 28 February 1994, while on a Deny Flight combat air patrol in a 555th Fighter Squadron (FS) Lockheed Martin F-16C Fighting Falcon. His wing man was Capt Scott O'Grady. *(Tim Ripley)*

British Royal Air Force SEPECAT Jaguar GR. Mk.1As saw action on two occasions in 1994 attacking a Serb armoured vehicle around Sarajevo in the summer and hitting Udbina airbase as part of the major NATO air strike in November. On both these occasions 1,000lb iron bombs were used with great accuracy. *(Tim Ripley)*

USAF McDonnell Douglas F-15E Strike Eagles, of the 492nd Fighter Squadron (FS), arrive at Aviano AB in February 1994 in the run-up to the Sarajevo heavy weapon exclusion zone ultimatum. They remained at the Italian base for a year, playing a major part in the air strikes of the following November. *(USAF/JCC(D))*

A Spanish *Ejercito del Aire* CASA C.212, of Ala (squadron) 37, was hit and badly damaged by a Serb heat-seeking surface-to-air missile in March 1994 while flying over Croatia. It managed to land safely. *(Tim Ripley)*

British Royal Air Force Panavia Tornado F.3 fighters maintained constant combat air patrols over Bosnia during 1994, operating from Gioia del Colle in southern Italy. A pair of Tornado F.3s had contact with two Serb SA-2 surface-to-air missiles (SAMs) in November. *(Tim Ripley)*

Close air support was the speciality of French *Armée de l'Air* Dassault Mirage F1CT, of 13e Escadre de Chasse (EC), which operated from Istrana, Italy. Their main weapon was the SAMP 250kg iron bomb, two were usually carried. *(Tim Ripley)*

French Army Aviation (ALAT) helicopter pilots braved hostile fire and other frustration at the hands of all warring factions to fly aid and casualty evacuation missions throughout war-torn Bosnia. Two French Pumas rescued British SAS Commandos from beseiged Gorazde in April 1994. *(Tim Ripley)*

Japanese diplomat Yasushi Akashi, who as Special Representative of the United Nations Secretary-General in the former Yugoslavia had the ultimate say over the use of NATO airpower. *(Tim Ripley)*

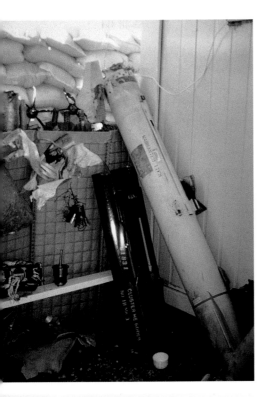

British Lieutenant General Sir Michael Rose, who angered US and Bosnian Muslim politicians by being too cautious in his use of airpower. He was much admired by UN troops under his command for keeping the UNPROFOR from getting sucked into the Bosnian war as a combatant. *(UNPROFOR)*

TOP LEFT:
The remains of an US AGM-88 High Speed Anti-Radiation Missile (HARM) fired near Bihac during November 1994. UN Military Observers recovered the weapon during a patrol after the Battle for Bihac. *(UNPROFOR/BHC)*

Target Udbina. USAF Lockheed Martin F-16C Fighting Falcons, of the 555th Fighter Squadron (FS), bombed up with CBU-87 cluster bombs, prepare to launch from Aviano AB, Italy, on 21 November 1994. The cluster weapons were used to put taxiways at the Serb-held airbase out of action. *(31st FW/A1C D. Lynn Walters)*

Mission accomplished. A USAF McDonnell Douglas F-15E Strike Eagle, of 492nd Fighter Squadron (FS), returns to Aviano AB, Italy after the Udbina strike with its bomb racks empty. The eight Strike Eagles that took part in the raid used 500lb GBU-12 laser guided bombs to blast craters in the Serb airbase's runways.
(31st FW/SSgt R 'Dixie' Trawick)

Udbina bound. USMC McDonnell Douglas F/A-18D Hornets, of Marine All Weather Fighter Attack Squadron (VMFA(AW)) 332, opened the strike on the Serb airbase by firing laser guided AGM-65 Maverick missiles and AGM-88 High Speed Anti-Radiation Missiles (HARMS) to take down the air defences around the target.
(31st FW/SSgt R 'Dixie' Trawick)

Heavy fighting around the eastern enclave of Gorazde almost led to the loss of a French *Aéronautique Navale* Dassault Etendard IVP photographic reconnaissance aircraft, of 16 Flotille (squadron) operating from the French Navy carrier *Clemenceau* in the Adriatic, when it was hit by a heat-seeking surface-to-air missile in April 1994. The aircraft was able to return safely to the carrier. *(Tim Ripley)*

Vital photographic intelligence was gathered by French *Armée de l'Air* Dassault Mirage F1CR, of 33e Escadre de Reconnaissance, based at Istrana in northern Italy. *(Tim Ripley)*

Sarajevo airport was constantly being closed during the year as fighting around the Bosnian capital flared into life.

To provide extra capability the British Royal Air Force SEPECAT Jaguar GR.Mk.1As flew in pairs during the reconnaissance missions, with one aircraft fitted with a LOROP pod and the other using a BAe F126 wide area general survey pod. *(Tim Ripley)*

The serpent insigina worn on French *Armée de l'Air* SEPECAT Jaguar As, of Escadron de Chasse 3/11, based at Istrana Italy, May 1994. *(Tim Ripley)*

The arms of Alsace insignia worn on French *Armée de l'Air* Dassault Mirage F1CTs of Escadron de Chasse 3/13, based at Istrana, Italy, May 1994. *(Tim Ripley)*

The seagull insignia worn on French *Armée de l'Air* Dassault Mirage F1CRs, of Escadron de Reconnaissance 2/33, based at Istrana, Italy, May 1994. *(Tim Ripley)*

The cat's face insignia worn on French *Armée de l'Air* SEPECAT Jaguar As, of Escadron de Chasse 3/11, based at Istrana, Italy, May 1994. *(Tim Ripley)*

CHAPTER 8
UN RAPID REACTION FORCE IS FORMED, SPRING/SUMMER 1995

The spring of 1995 saw fighting break out again on a large scale. The Bosnian Army had scored local successes against the Serbs north of Tuzla and on Mount Vlassic near Zenica. The Serbs responded by escalating the conflict around Sarajevo and taking back many of their tanks and artillery from the UN weapon collection points. On 8 April a USAF Lockheed Martin C-130E Hercules approaching Sarajevo airport was racked by machine gun fire. While the aircraft was able to take off safely the UNHCR closed the airlift down and it would not reopen for six months. The new UN commander in Bosnia, Lieutenant General Rupert Smith, again called in NATO jets to buzz the city in the hope of calming the situation. This time the Serbs called the UN's bluff and kept on fighting.

General Smith upped the ante and ordered NATO to bomb Serb ammunition dumps near their self-styled capital Pale on 25 May. USAF Lockheed Martin F-16C Fighting Falcons and Spanish *Ejercito del Aire* McDonnell Douglas EF-18A+ Hornets hit the target with laser guided bombs, raising a massive mushroom cloud over the city. The Serbs did not back down, shelling Tuzla and killing 75 civilians. More NATO aircraft attacked the Pale ammunition dumps. This time the Serbs decided to take 300 UN personnel hostage and they were filmed by Pale TV chained to military installations. Western governments ordered General Smith to cool it. The British and French Governments then decided to create a heavily armed Rapid Reaction Force (RRF) to give UNPROFOR more flexibility to deal with any of the warring factions that might try to interfere with its operations. It would take time for the RRF to get in place so the UN would have to cope with its in-place forces 'until the cavalry arrived'. The British decided to give UNPROFOR its own artillery regiment and the RAF Hercules force flew up to 14 sorties a day into Split to bring in the guns in a week.

As UN commanders entered delicate negotiations to get their hostages back from the Serbs. The USAF almost provided them with an additional guest when an F-16 was shot down by an SA-6 radar guided surface-to-air missile (SAM) over western Bosnia. The pilot, Captain Scott O'Grady, evaded capture for six days before allied aircraft picked up his radio transmissions and a rescue mission was launched. A large package of NATO aircraft protected the rescue force of US Marine Corps helicopters launched from the USS *Kearsarge*. The two Bell AH-1W Super Cobras and two Sikorsky CH-53E Sea Stallions found O'Grady and managed to lift him to safety after dodging SA-7 heat-seeking SAMs over Krajina.

The British and French were finalising plans to move the two-brigade strong Rapid Reaction Force into Bosnia via Croatian ports and airports. However, they faced strong opposition from the Croats who did not want the RRF to obstruct their planned offensive against the Serb-held Krajina. While the Bosnians thought the RRF would be used to cover a UN withdrawal, leaving them at the mercy of the Serbs and Croats, the Croats demanded massive fees for the use of their facilities and the Bosnians delayed permission for the RRF to cross into their territory.

These delays meant that when Serb forces started to launch a major offensive against the Muslim enclave of Srebrenica in early July, the UN was badly placed to do anything about it. At the 5th Allied Tactical Air Force (5 ATAF) in Vicenza, NATO air commanders were expecting trouble and each day they put up a strike package over the Adriatic ready to intervene. On 11 July NATO jets made sweeps over the town as Serb tanks advanced. Two Royal Netherlands Air Force F-16As attacked hitting a Serb tank, bunker and command post.

The outnumbered Dutch troops were only just able to extract themselves from the trap and make their way to a UN base outside the town. The 24,000 Muslims in the town were now at the mercy of Serbs and many thousands are believed to have been massacred. Thousands of others fled to Tuzla, where the UNHCR pressed two Ukrainian Air Force Mil Mi-26 heavy lift helicopters into service to fly in humanitarian aid for the refugees.

On 3 July the USAF was finally able to begin Operation Quick Lift to fly in personnel of the British Army's 24 Airmobile Brigade to Split. It took a month to fly in the 1,700 strong addition to the RRF, with Lockheed C-141 Starlifters and C-5 Galaxys flying some 60 missions from RAF Brize Norton in the UK.

The RRF set up a new heliport at the Croatian port of Ploce ready for the arrival of additional helicopters. The French Army Aviation's (ALAT) 5e Regiment d'Helicopter de Combat brought eight Aérospatiale Gazelle attack and seven Aérospatiale SA330B Puma transport helicopters. While the aviation component of the British airmobile brigade was made up of 3 Regiment Army Air Corps with nine Westland Lynx AH.7, nine Lynx AH.9 and nine Gazelles, and the RAF Support Helicopter Force with six Boeing Chinook HC.2s and six Puma HC.1s. Until the launch of Operation Deliberate Force at the end of August the Bosnian government refused to allow green painted RRF helicopters to fly into their airspace. The only UN helicopters that could fly in Bosnia were its 'white' painted ones.

Croatian troops launched Operation Storm to drive the Serbs from the Krajina region on 4 August and on the same day Krajina Serb radar illuminated US Navy jets, who responded by firing AGM-88 High Speed Anti-radiation missiles at the site. In the wake of the Croatian offensive, some 150,000 Serb refugees fled into Bosnia, leading to the UNHCR organising an airlift of aid from its Ancona depot to Belgrade by chartered Ilyushin Il-76s. Roads in northern Bosnia, however, were so clogged with refugees that the aid could not get through by truck. The RAF therefore deployed two Chinooks to the main UN base at Pleso Camp, outside Zagreb, to fly aid to Banja Luka.

After the débâcle at Srebrenica and the UN-organised evacuation of Zepa, the British, French and the American governments resolved to protect the remaining UN safe areas with widespread air strikes and ground units of the RRF. NATO and UN planners put the finishing touches to contingency plans to strike back at the Bosnian Serbs. All that was required was another outrage to trigger the response. It would not take long for the crisis to reach a climax.

USAF General Dynamics EF-111A Raven jamming aircraft, of the 429th Electronic Combat Squadron (ECS), spent much of 1995 at Aviano AB, Italy, providing jamming protection for Operation Deny Flight patrols over Bosnia because of the continuing Serb radar-guided surface-to-air missile (SAM) threat. *(Tim Ripley)*

After the UN Rapid Reaction Force (RRF) moved its artillery on to Mount Igman at the end of July 1995 to protect the convoy routes into Sarajevo, British, Norwegian and French helicopters had to daily dodge fire from Bosnian and Serb troops to support the UN force. A number of helicopters were hit and had to limp to safety at the UN helicopter landing site at Kiseljak. *(Tim Ripley)*

RIGHT AND OPPOSITE:
Westland Lynx AH.Mk.9s, of the British Army's 3 Regiment, Army Air Corps, provided battlefield mobility for the infantry of 24 Airmobile Brigade after it deployed to Ploce Dockyard Camp in August 1995. Like the French counterparts, the British helicopter crews were not able to enter Bosnian air space until after the start of Operation Deliberate Force. In October 1995 the British government announced 24 Airmobile Brigade would be withdrawing to the UK. *(Tim Ripley)*

Ukrainian Air Force Mil Mi-26 heavy lift helicopters assigned to UN Peace Force (UNPF) deployed to Split and Tuzla in July to ferry aid to refugees from the fallen UN 'safe area' of Srebrenica. After Serb defeats in September and October the Mi-26s moved to Zagreb to fly aid to Serb refugees around Banja Luka. *(Tim Ripley)*

OPPOSITE AND BELOW:
664 Squadron, Army Air Corps, arrived in Bosnia from Britain in January 1995 with four Westland Lynx AH.Mk.7s to provide mobility for UN troops establishing a ceasefire agreement. After the hostage crisis of May 1995, the squadron was attached to the newly established UN Rapid Reaction Force (RRF) providing mobility for senior commanders and surveillance. *(Tim Ripley)*

The involvement of Spanish *Ejercito del Aire* McDonnell Douglas F/A-18A+ Hornets, of Ala (Wing) 12, in the May 1995 air strikes on the Serb ammunition dumps at Pale, was the first combat missions by the Spaniards since the civil war in the 1930s. The Spaniards first deployed to Aviano AB, Italy, in late November 1994, with eight Hornets of Ala 15 and two Lockheed Martin KC-130H, of Ala 31. Most of the Ala 15 contingent rotated back to Spain in the spring of 1995 except for a small Hornet contingent for suppression of enemy air defence (SEAD) tasks with AGM-88 High Speed Anti-Radiation Missiles (HARM). *(Tim Ripley)*

USMC McDonnell Douglas F/A-18D Hornets, of Marine All Weather Fighter Attack Squadron (VMFA(AW)) 533, took part in all the major air operations of the summer of 1995: the air raids on Pale in May, the rescue of downed USAF pilot Capt Scott O'Grady in June and Operation Deliberate Force. *(Tim Ripley)*

A British Royal Navy Westland Sea King HC.4, of 845 Squadron, carrying a 105mm howitzer to a firing position during a UN Rapid Reaction Force training exercise in July 1995 at Tomislavgrad, western Bosnia.
(UKLF Media Production Cell)

To provide humanitarian aid to Serb refugees from the Croatian offensive in the Krajina region, two 'white'-painted British Royal Air Force Boeing Chinook HC.Mk.2 support helicopters, of 7 Squadron, were flown out to Pleso airport, near Zagreb, in August to begin airlifting supplies to Banja Luka. Not surprisingly the aid operation ended as soon a NATO started its air strikes against the Bosnian Serbs later in the month.
(RAF Strike Command/Cpl John Cassidy)

The shooting down of a 555th Fighter Squadron (FS) Lockheed Martin F-16C Fighting Falcon on 2 June 1995 caused a major crisis while the pilot, a certain Captain Scott O'Grady, was on the run in Serb-held territory. He was rescued by a USMC helicopter force six days later to much celebration. *(Tim Ripley)*

The British Royal Navy 801 Squadron, embarked on HMS *Illustrious*, was the first unit to take the BAe Sea Harrier F/A.2 on a full operational tour in the Adriatic, off the former Yugoslavia in February 1995. *(Andrew Wray/BAe/via Peter March)*

CHAPTER 9
OPERATION DELIBERATE FORCE, AUTUMN 1995

Sarajevo rocked with explosions and the night was lit-up with decoy flares dropped by NATO strike aircraft. Operation Deliberate Force had begun. The trigger for the unleashing of NATO airpower was a mortar attack on a Sarajevo market which killed 38 civilians on 28 August 1995. The UN announced that the round had been fired from Bosnian Serb positions. This then opened the way for the 'disproportionate' use of airpower by NATO in line with the new-found resolve of Britain, France and the United States to defend the remaining UN 'safe areas'.

Within 24 hours the commander of UN Peace Forces in the former Yugoslavia, French Lieutenant General Bernard Janvier, and NATO's Allied Forces South European (AFSOUTH) commander made a 'dual key' decision to execute their contingency response, Operation Deliberate Force. Planners at the 5th Allied Tactical Air Force (5 ATAF) at Vicenza, in Italy, quickly confirmed details of the joint air-ground assault with the UNPROFOR Headquarters in Sarajevo and the Operations Staff of the UN Rapid Reaction Force (RRF) outside the city at Kiseljak. The operation would begin no earlier than 0200hrs on 30 August. In Italy and on aircraft carriers in the Adriatic, allied airmen and ground crews were already preparing for the crucial first strike.

Dead-Eye South East

To clear the way for the main strike force, US Navy McDonnell Douglas F/A-18C Hornets and Grumman EA-6B Prowlers, launched from the aircraft carrier USS *Theodore Roosevelt* attacked the Serb integrated air defence system (IADS) around Sarajevo under the code-name 'Dead-Eye South East'. They hit radar sites, command posts, communications towers and surface-to-air missile (SAM) sites with laser guided bombs and AGM-88 High Speed Anti-Radiation Missiles (HARM) that homed in on radar signals. USAF Lockheed Martin EC-130H Compass Call and General Dynamics EF-111A Raven jamming aircraft supported the raid by blinding Serb communications and radars.

An hour later the first of five strike packages were sent into action over the city and attacked ammunition dumps, barracks, artillery positions and other key military targets for the remainder of the day. The raids, by packages of up to 30 strike aircraft at a time, were carried out predominately with laser guided bombs to achieve maximum accuracy and minimum collateral damage. RRF artillery on Mount Igman joined in the assault and kept the pressure on the Serbs in between air strikes. USAF Lockheed Martin EC-130E Airborne Battlefield Command and Control Centre (ABCCC) aircraft were in the air throughout the operation to act as the link between air and ground forces. The ABCCC also played a key role in co-ordinating the in-bound strike packages and often re-tasked them in the air to secondary targets if the first wave of an attack force reported they had destroyed the primary targets.

NATO suffered its only combat loss of the operation when a French *Armée de l'Air* Dassault Mirage 2000K-2 was hit by a Serb SAM while bombing Pale. The two crew were quickly captured by the Serbs and held hostage until December. Three rescue missions involving US Navy and USAF Special Operation Forces helicopters were launched but the Frenchmen had already been captured by the Bosnian Serbs.

On 31 August three more strike packages were sent into action before the operation was put on hold. The aim was to see if the Serbs would agree to UN and NATO demands for them to pull back their heavy weapons from around Sarajevo.

Bombing resumes

The Bosnian Serb commander, General Ratko Mladic, refused to blink and NATO resumed its offensive air operations at 1000hrs on 5 September. With most targets in the Sarajevo region now smoking ruins, 5 ATAF began to expand the scope of its operations hitting bridges, IADS sites, ammunition dumps, command posts and barracks further out from the city.

Up to seven strike packages were flown daily, by day and night. Each package was a multi-national effort mixing aircraft with different capabilities to achieve the objective. At all times AWACS, fighter, close air support (CAS), suppression of enemy air defence (SEAD) and photographic reconnaissance aircraft were in the air to support the strike aircraft and UN troops on the ground. Tankers were kept in tracks over the Adriatic to refuel the airborne armada around the clock. German and Italian Panavia Tornados now joined the operations, with the *Aeronautica Militare Italiana* aircraft flying bombing missions and the *Luftwaffe* conducting SEAD and photographic reconnaissance tasks .

On 9 September, the operation was significantly expanded when IADS targets in north west Bosnia around Banja Luka were attacked with stand-off weapons, such as GBU-15 2,000lb glide bomb and AGM-84 Stand-Off Land Attack Missiles (SLAMs), which could be launched from outside the firing envelopes of long range Serb SA-6 SAMs. The following day the US Navy fired 13 Tomahawk Land Attack Missiles (TLAMs) against more targets around Banja Luka. Serb artillery near Tuzla now opened fire on UN Nordic troops based near the city. They requested 'Blue Sword', or close air support, to silence the guns and three flights of US Marine Corps Hornets from the USS *America* were soon overhead. They silenced the guns and two command posts with laser guided bombs.

This high tempo of operations was maintained by 5 ATAF over the next three days but the target list was slowly becoming exhausted due to the heavy damage inflicted to date. By 13 September bad weather was increasingly restricting operations because good weather was needed for most laser guided weapons to be fully effective. The next day the UN and NATO put their offensive operations on hold after General Mladic signalled he was ready to agree to pull back his heavy weapons from Sarajevo, open road and air routes into the city, and agree a ceasefire around the Bosnian capital.

Ops continue

On 15 September a French *Armée de l'Air* Lockheed Martin C-130H Hercules landed at Sarajevo to reopen the UNHCR airbridge after a six month stand down. The British, Canadian, German and US aircraft started their operations from Ancona the following day. NATO fighters provided close escort to the airlifters, who used fully tactical 'Khe Sanh' approaches to minimise the opportunity for anyone to fire upon them. General Janvier and Admiral Smith flew into Sarajevo on 20 September to review the situation and declared Deliberate Force had met its objectives, so 'the resumption of air strikes is currently not necessary'.

This was not the end of NATO air operations over Bosnia since fighting continued in the west of the country where the Bosnians and Croats had launched a major offensive. The Serbs mobilised their air force at Banja Luka to help turn the tide but 5 ATAF ordered NATO fighters into the area to enforce the no-fly zone. Heavy SEAD patrols were on hand to protect the allied fighters from Serb SAMs.

US Marine Corps EA-6B Prowlers on patrol over western Bosnia and near Sarajevo were illuminated by Serb radars on 4 October. They responded by firing HARM missiles at the threats. A more serious situation developed four days later near Tuzla when the Serbs fired a multi-barrelled rocket launcher at Bosnian troops. UN Nordic troops were caught in the cross-fire and one peacekeeper was killed. 'Blue Sword' was again called into action but the NATO jets could not find their targets as nightfall approached. A major strike against the Serb positions was organised for the following day and they were blasted with laser guided bombs.

During the 17 days of Deliberate Force, NATO aircraft flew some 3,515 sorties of which 1,372 were close air support or battle-field air interdiction involving the dropping of bombs. A further 785 SEAD sorties were tasked against Serb air defences. Some 708 precision guided munitions were used with a high degree of accuracy and just over 300 'iron' or 'dump' bombs were also used. There were 56 HARM missiles fired and more than 10,000 rounds of cannon ammunition fired by USAF Lockheed Martin AC-130H Spectre gunships and Fairchild A-10A Warthogs.

The air bombardment of the Serbs dramatically altered the strategic balance in Bosnia, since the Serbs found their advantage in heavy weapons, communications and air power had been neutralised. Within days of Deliberate Force being concluded the Croats and Bosnians drove the Serbs from large areas of western Bosnia. The combination of Deliberate Force and their defeats in the west forced the Bosnian Serb leadership to sign up to the Dayton Peace accords in November, thus opening the way for the deployment of NATO's Peace Implementation Force (IFOR) to police the new peace.

Spanish *Ejercito del Aire* McDonnell Douglas EF-18A+ Hornets, of 12 and 15 (wings) Ala, flew just under a 100 sorties during Deliberate Force using 1,000lb GBU-16 laser guided bombs to blast Serb targets and AGM-88 High Speed Anti-Radiation Missiles to protect allied aircraft from hostile surface-to-air missile (SAM) threats. *(USAF/JJC(D))*

Serb air defences were suppressed during Deliberate Force by US Navy and Marine Corps Grumman EA-6B Prowler electronic warfare aircraft from five squadrons, which were either based at Aviano or afloat on carriers in the Adriatic. Navy Tactical Electronic Warfare Squadron (VAQ) 130, 141 and 209, as well as Marine Tactical Electronic Warfare Squadron (VMAQ) 1 and 3, all found themselves protecting allied aircraft during the period of NATO offensive air operations. *(USAF/JJC(D))*

2,000lb GBU-10 Paveway laser guided bombs being prepared for action at Aviano AB, Italy. Some 344 of the weapons were built from kits by Aviano's bomb dump ready for use during Deliberate Force. In total 440 tons of bombs worth $12.5 million were dropped by Aviano-based USAF aircraft. *(USAF/JJC(D))*

Putting precision guided weapons on target was the job of the McDonnell Douglas F-15E Strike Eagles, of the 494th Fighter Squadron (FS), which were called upon to hit key Serb targets. Flying just over 100 sorties from Aviano, AB, Italy, the Strike Eagles used Paveway laser guided bombs against targets around Sarajevo and eight stand-off GBU-15 electro-optical weapons to take out air defence sites deep behind Serb lines in north-west Bosnia. *(USAF/JJC(D))*

Aviano AB's two Lockheed Martin F-16C
Fighting Falcon squadrons, the 510th and
555th Fighter Squadrons (FS), bore the
brunt of the allied strike effort during
Deliberate Force to fly more than 350
sorties, using only laser guided bombs,
designated by their on-board LANTIRN
pods. (USAF/JJC(D))

To stop the Bosnian Serb air force taking to the air after Deliberate Force NATO fighters, including British Royal Air Force Panavia Tornados flown by No 111 Squadron, mounted intense combat air patrols over north-west Bosnia. The Serbs got the message and kept on the ground when the NATO jets were overhead.
(Tim Ripley)

The target designation of laser guided bombs was carried out by the British Royal Air Force's BAe Harrier GR.7s, SEPECAT Jaguar GR.Mk.1Bs, of No 54 Squadron, equipped with the thermal imaging airborne laser designation (TIALD) pods, were deployed to Italy in August 1995. A pair of Harriers were usually accompanied by a single Jaguar, which would find the targets and then guide the Harrier's bombs until they impacted.
(CPRO/ HQ RAF Strike Command)

OPPOSITE PAGE:
Royal Netherlands Air Force Lockheed Martin F-16A Fighting Falcons, of 322 and 306 Squadrons, were in the thick of the action during Deliberate Force flying 198 missions delivering unguided 'iron' bombs with great accuracy. Almost half the Dutch missons were photographic reconnaissance missions to hunt out new targets and provide bomb damage assessment intelligence. *(Tim Ripley)*

Hornet Strike – USS *America*. The three McDonnell Douglas F/A-18C Hornet squadrons embarked on the USS *America* – Navy Strike Fighter Squadrons (VFA) 82 and 86, and Marine Fighter Attack Squadron (VMFA) 251 – began air strikes over Bosnia from 10 September, delivering some 30 laser guided bombs and firing three AGM-84 Stand-Off Land Attack Missiles (SLAMS) against Serb targets throughout Bosnia. *(Tim Ripley)*

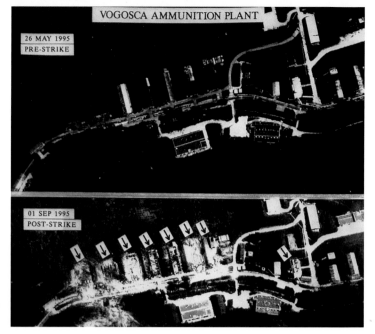

The accuracy of NATO precision guided munitions can be judged from these aerial reconnaissance photographs taken before and after Operation Deliberate Force air strikes by the *Armée de l'Air*. *(US DoD)*

Mission accomplished. On 15 September the first UNHCR aircraft for six months touched down at Sarajevo airport when the Bosnian Serb military leadership gave in to UN demands after Deliberate Force. British Royal Air Force Lockheed Martin Hercules HC1P, of 47 Squadron, began flying into Sarajevo on 16 September. *(Tim Ripley)*

To jam Serb air defence radio communications systems three Lockheed Martin EC-130H Compass Call jamming aircraft, of the 43rd Electronic Combat Squadron (ECS), were deployed to Aviano AB, Italy, for Deliberate Force. They orbited outside Bosnia air space radiating power-jamming signals to blind Serb fighter and surface-to-air missile control radio networks.
(Tim Ripley)

Throughout Deliberate Force a USAF McDonnell Douglas KC-10A Extender, of the 9th Air Refuelling Squadron (ARS), was airborne in a tanker track over the Adriatic, passing fuel to US and allied aircraft. Because the giant tankers possessed both boom and probe/drogue refuelling systems they could pass fuel to every type of aircraft taking part in the operation, making them a highly flexible asset. Often Boeing KC-135 Stratotankers would pass fuel to the Extenders, to allow them to pass on fuel to fighters that had incompatible refuelling systems with the veteran Boeing tanker. *(Tim Ripley)*

Photographic reconnaissance gathering was the main task of US Navy Grumman F-14A Tomcats, of Fighter Squadron (VF) 102, using their TARPS pods. Photographic imagery of targets was vital to allow aircrew using forward-looking infra-red vision devices to recognise their targets and then direct laser guided bombs on to them. *(Tim Ripley)*

Crowded skies. NATO fighters line up behind McDonnell Douglas KC-10A Extender, of the 9th Air Refuelling Squadron (ARS) during Deliberate Force. Fighter pilots had to stick strictly to the air refuelling plan otherwise they could create traffic jams behind the tankers, causing aircraft to miss their 'time-on-target'.
(Tim Ripley)

1,000lb GBU-16 laser guided bombs were used extensively by Spanish *Ejercito del Aire* McDonnell Douglas F/A-18C Hornets during Operation Deliberate Force. *(Tim Ripley)*

Waiting for the call. A British Royal Air Force BAe Harrier GR.7, of No 4 Squadron, on close air support alert at Gioia del Colle. During Deliberate Force the Harrier detachment were employed delivering 1,000lb Paveway laser guided bombs on Serb targets, with SEPECAT Jaguar GR.Mk.2Bs, of No 54 Squadron, providing laser designation with their thermal imaging airborne laser designation (TIALD) pods. *(Jeremy Flack/API)*

Joint strike packages involving aircraft from all the NATO nations participating in Operation Deliberate Force were the norm. Here a French *Armée de l'Air* Dassault Mirage 2000D, of 3 Escadre de Chasse (EC) is working with a Royal Netherlands Air Force 322 Squadron Lockheed Martin F-16A Fighting Falcon. *(Tim Ripley)*

CHAPTER 10
NATO TAKES OVER, DECEMBER 1995

On 20 December 1995, NATO's Peace Implementation (IFOR) took over responsibility from the UN for keeping the peace in Bosnia-Herzegovina and so bring to the end Operation Deny Flight and other UN associated air operations. The UNHCR airlift to Sarajevo continued through to the following January but almost 1,000 days of continuous air support for UNPROFOR were at an end. The 5th Allied Tactical Air Force (5 ATAF) itself became the air component of IFOR and continued its patrols but the rules of the game were now very different.

NATO flew just over 100,000 sorties up until December 1995, of which 23,021 were combat air patrols enforcing the no-fly zone, and 27,077 were close air support and air strike sorties. Some 29,158 were support missions by tankers, electronic warfare, AWACS and reconnaissance sorties and there were an additional 21,164 training sorties carried out over Italy and the Adriatic

The UNPROFOR mission and its supporting NATO air operations were the subject of intense scrutiny from the international media and some politicians, who were very quick to criticise and second guess the commanders on the spot. Given that until August 1995 Western political leaders had refused to sanction a military solution to force the warring parties to the negotiating table, UNPROFOR and NATO were only allowed to pursue limited military, political and humanitarian objectives with very limited resources. Events of the early summer of 1995 indicated that a radical re-assessment of Western policy was needed. At last London, Paris and Washington agreed to conduct decisive military operations to force a peace.

Airpower was a key component in all UN and NATO operations in the former Yugoslavia. The 12,951 UNHCR aid airlift into Sarajevo kept the people of the city alive through three terrible years of seige and the 2,828 airdrop missions fed the enclaves for two winters. UNPROFOR's own 'white' air force flew thousands of sorties into Sarajevo bringing aid and supplies for its peacekeepers. Along with the UNHCR assigned aircraft, UNPROFOR's aircraft and helicopters evacuated countless wounded UN soldiers and Bosnian civilians to safety outside the war zone. International diplomats relied on the UN and UNHCR aircraft in their numerous attempts to broker a peace deal. During three and half years of war, the presence overhead of NATO strike aircraft deterred attacks on UN aid convoys and peacekeepers on countless occasions. These operations attracted little attention but UN soldiers knew the presence of NATO bombers was very intimidating to Bosnian warlords. Also the combat air patrols of Deny Flight and air strike on Udbina effectively kept the Bosnian and Krajina Serb air forces out of the war except for minor pin-prick hit-and-run attacks of little consequence.

When NATO airpower was finally unleashed it too proved to be a decision factor in forcing the warring factions to come to the negotiating table and be ready to talk in good faith. They knew the punishing air strikes would resume if they reneged on these new agreements. Things were now very different from the early days of the conflict when the warring factions regularly treated UN or European Union negotiators with open contempt. The political will to employ airpower was the key to its successful use in the four-year-long bloody Bosnian conflict.

The success of Operation Deliberate Force opened the way for the deployment of NATO's Implementation Force (IFOR), and the arrival of 20,000 US ground troops at Tuzla airbase in north-east Bosnia.
(Tim Ripley)

Operation Joint Endeavor, the deployment of IFOR to Bosnia saw the first major operational use of the USAF's new McDonnell Douglas C-17A Globemaster III airlifter. The aircraft carried thousands of US troops and hundreds of heavy armoured vehicles from bases in Germany to Tuzla, in Bosnia. *(Tim Ripley)*

APPENDIX A
NATO/UN CHAIN OF COMMAND
AUGUST/SEPTEMBER 1995

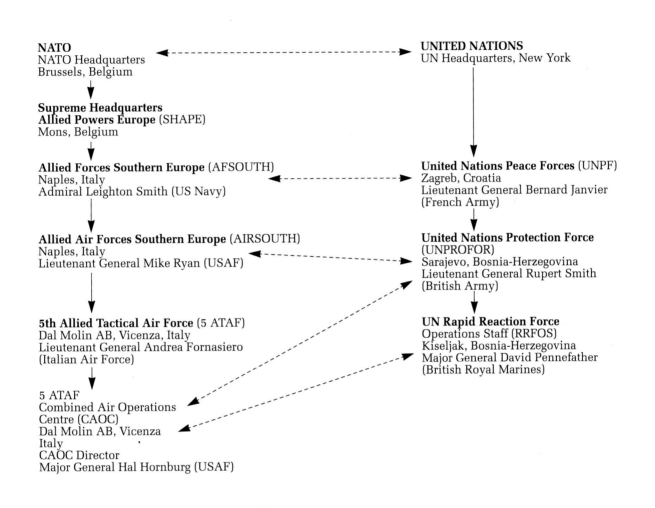

NATO
NATO Headquarters
Brussels, Belgium

**Supreme Headquarters
Allied Powers Europe** (SHAPE)
Mons, Belgium

Allied Forces Southern Europe (AFSOUTH)
Naples, Italy
Admiral Leighton Smith (US Navy)

Allied Air Forces Southern Europe (AIRSOUTH)
Naples, Italy
Lieutenant General Mike Ryan (USAF)

5th Allied Tactical Air Force (5 ATAF)
Dal Molin AB, Vicenza, Italy
Lieutenant General Andrea Fornasiero
(Italian Air Force)

5 ATAF
Combined Air Operations
Centre (CAOC)
Dal Molin AB, Vicenza
Italy
CAOC Director
Major General Hal Hornburg (USAF)

UNITED NATIONS
UN Headquarters, New York

United Nations Peace Forces (UNPF)
Zagreb, Croatia
Lieutenant General Bernard Janvier
(French Army)

United Nations Protection Force
(UNPROFOR)
Sarajevo, Bosnia-Herzegovina
Lieutenant General Rupert Smith
(British Army)

UN Rapid Reaction Force
Operations Staff (RRFOS)
Kiseljak, Bosnia-Herzegovina
Major General David Pennefather
(British Royal Marines)

Note: On 1 April 1995 the UN mandate in Croatia was revised and UNPROFOR ceased to be the generic term for all UN troops in the former Yugoslavia and the term UN Peace Forces (UNPF) was adopted . The old UN Bosnia-Herzegovina Command (BHC) adopted the title UNPROFOR, while UN in Croatia became the United Nations Restoration Operation in Croatia (UNCRO) and the operation in Macedonia became the United Nations Preventative Deployment Force (UNPREDEP).

Appendix B
UN/UNHCR/NATO Air Operation Staffs, August 1995

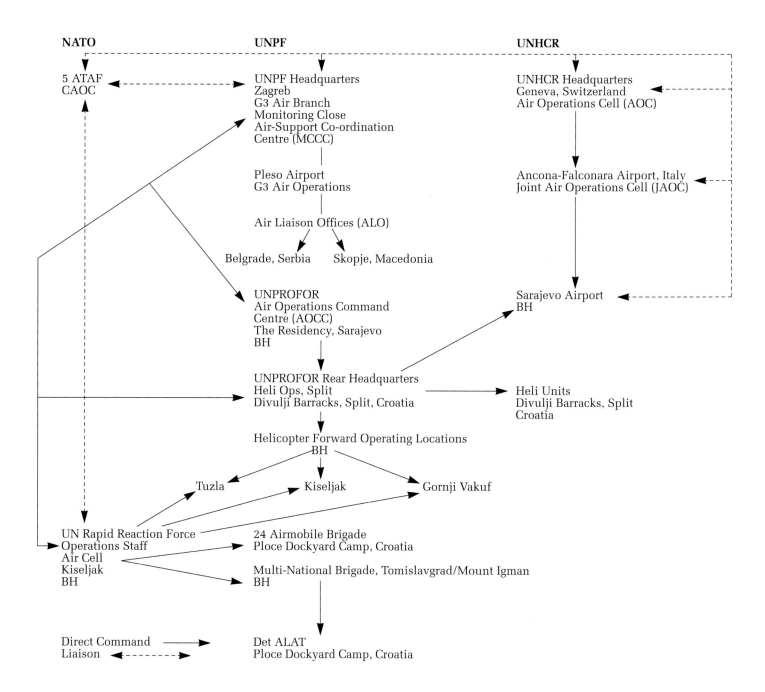

NATO

5 ATAF
CAOC

UN Rapid Reaction Force
Operations Staff
Air Cell
Kiseljak
BH

Direct Command
Liaison

UNPF

UNPF Headquarters
Zagreb
G3 Air Branch
Monitoring Close
Air-Support Co-ordination
Centre (MCCC)

Pleso Airport
G3 Air Operations

Air Liaison Offices (ALO)

Belgrade, Serbia   Skopje, Macedonia

UNPROFOR
Air Operations Command
Centre (AOCC)
The Residency, Sarajevo
BH

UNPROFOR Rear Headquarters
Heli Ops, Split
Divulji Barracks, Split, Croatia

Helicopter Forward Operating Locations
BH

Tuzla   Kiseljak   Gornji Vakuf

24 Airmobile Brigade
Ploce Dockyard Camp, Croatia

Multi-National Brigade, Tomislavgrad/Mount Igman
BH

Det ALAT
Ploce Dockyard Camp, Croatia

UNHCR

UNHCR Headquarters
Geneva, Switzerland
Air Operations Cell (AOC)

Ancona-Falconara Airport, Italy
Joint Air Operations Cell (JAOC)

Sarajevo Airport
BH

Heli Units
Divulji Barracks, Split
Croatia

APPENDIX C
UN/NATO AIR ORDER OF BATTLE, AUGUST–SEPTEMBER 1995

BASE	UNIT	NUMBER	AIRCRAFT
CANADA			
Ancona		1	CC-130
Sigonella	405, 407		
	415 Sqns	2	CC-140
FRANCE			
Cervia	EC3/5	6	Mirage 2000C
	EC2/3	3	Mirage 2000K-2
	EC1/3	4	Mirage 2000D
Istrana	EC2/33	5	Mirage F-1CR
	EC3/11	8	Jaguar
Istres	ERV93	1	KC-135R
Avord	ED36	1	E-3F Sentry
Vicenza	EET11/54	1	C-160D
		1	Nord 262
Evreux	EE51	1	DC-8
Sigonella/Elmas			Atlantic
Split-Divulji Det ALAT		6	Puma
/Kiseljak (3 RHC/4RHCM)		4	Gazelle
Ploce	5 RHC	8	Gazelle
		7	Puma
Ancona	ET2/61	1	C-130H/H-30
Brindisi	EH67	3	Puma
Mont de Marsan	EB91		Mirage IV
GERMANY			
Sigonella/Elmas	MFG3		Atlantic MPA
Nordholz	MFG2	2	Atlantic SIGINT
Ancona	LTG61	1	C-160D
Piacenza J	BG32	8	Tornado ECR
	AG51	6	Tornado IDS
ITALY			
Ghedi	6 Stormo	8	Tornado IDS
Gioia del Colle	36 Stormo	8	Tornado IDS
Pisa	48 Brigata	4	G222
		1	C-130
Istrana	51 Stormo	6	AMX
NATO AIRBORNE EARLY WARNING FORCE			
Gelienkirken/Trapani/Previza		8	E-3A Sentry
NETHERLANDS			
Sigonelle	320/321 Sqn	?	P-3
Villafranca	322 Sqn	13	F-16A
	306 Sqn	5	F-16A(R)
NORWAY			
Tuzla	720 Sqn	4	Arapahos

BASE	UNIT	NUMBER	AIRCRAFT
PORTUGAL			
Sigonella	601 Sqn	?	P-3P
SPAIN			
Aviano	311 Sqn	2	KC-130
	12/15 Ala	8	EF-18A+
Sigonella	221 Sqn	?	P-3B
Vicenza	37 Sqn	1	CASA 212
TURKEY			
Ghedi	191 Sqn	18	F-16C
UKRAINE			
Split		2	Mi-26
Zagreb-Pleso		3	Mi-8TV
UNITED NATIONS PEACE FORCES (civil contract aircraft)			
Pleso-Zagreb		2	Il-76
		1	Tu-154
		2	Yak-40
		2	Bell 212
		1	Bell 206
Skopje		1	Bell 212
		2	Bell 206
UNITED KINGDOM			
Gioia del Colle	4 Sqn	12	Harrier GR.7
	54 Sqn	2	Jaguar GR.1B
	111 Sqn	6	Tornado F.3
	No1 PRU	1	Canberra PR.9
Palermo	216 Sqn	2	TriStar
Aviano	8 Sqn	2	E-3D Sentry
Sigonella	Kinloss Wing	?	Nimrod MR.2P
Pratica di Mare	51 Sqn	?	Nimrod R.2P
Ancona	47 Sqn SF Flt	1	Hercules HC1P
HMS *Invincible*	800 Sqn	6	Sea Harrier F/A.2
	814 Sqn	7	Sea King HAS.6
	849 Sqn	3	Sea King AEW.Mk.2
Ploce	7 Sqn	6	Chinook HC.2
	33 Sqn	6	Puma HC.1
	3 Regt AAC	9	Lynx AH.7
		9	Lynx AH.9
		9	Gazelle
Split-Divulji	661 Sqn AAC	6	Lynx AH.7
/Gornji Vakuf	845 Sqn	4	Sea King HC.4
Zagreb-Pleso	RAF SHF	2	Chinook HC.2
(returned UK end Aug 95)			

BASE	UNIT	NUMBER	AIRCRAFT
UNITED STATES			
Aviano –	7490th (Provisional) Wing		
	31st Fighter Wing		
	494th FS	8	F-15E
	VFMA(AW)-533	12	F /A-18D
	(replaced by VFMA-224 15/9/95)		
	510th FS	24	F-16C
	555th FS	24	F-16C
	104th FG	12	O/A-10A
	42nd ACCS	4	EC-130E. ABCCC
	43rd ECS	3	EC-130H Compass Call
	429th ECS	6	EF-111A
	23rd FS	8	F-16C HTS
	E Coy 502nd Avn Bn	16	CH-47D
	VAQ-130/141/209	2-5	EA-6B
	VMAQ-1/3	2-5	EA-6B
	(EA-6Bs rotated through Aviano on a daily basis)		
Ancona	37th AS Det	2	C-130E
Sigonella	VP-6/NP-62	8	P-3C
Pisa	91st ARS	6	KC-135R
	(Det 2, 100th ARW)		
Istres	712nd ARS(to 31/8)	6	KC-135R
	99th ARS(from 1/9)		
	(Det 3, 100th ARW)		
Bari	HC-4 Det	2	CH-53E
Brindisi	21st SOS/20th SOS	7	MH-53J
	67th SOS/19th SOS?	4	HC-130P
	16th SOS	4	AC-130H
Rota/Souda Bay	VQ-2	5	EP-3E
	USNR TDY Det	2	P-3C
Mildenhall	55th Wing Det	?	RC-135
	351st ARS	9	KC-135R
Fairford/Cyprus	th RW Det	3/4	U-2R
Capodinichino	86th Wing?	2	C-21
Genoa	9th ARS	5	KC-10A
	(Det 10, 100th ARW)		

BASE	UNIT	AIRCRAFT
USS *Theodore Roosevelt*		
	VF-41	F-14A
	VFA-15	F/A-18C
	VFA-87	F/A-18C
	VMFA-312	F/A-18C
	VAW-124	EC-2C
	VAQ-141	EA-6B
	HS-3	H/SH-60F/H
	VS-24	S-3B
	VQ-6 Det D	ES-3A
(departed Adriatic 12.9.95)		
USS *America*		
	VF-102	F-14A
	VMFA-251	F/A-18C
	VFA-82	F/A-18C
	VFA-86	F/A-18C
	VAW-123	EC-2C
	VMAQ-3	EA-6B
	HS-11	H/SH-60F/H
	VS-32	S-3B
	VQ-6 Det A	ES-3A
(arrived Adriatic 9.9.95)		

BASE	UNIT	NUMBER	AIRCRAFT
Camp Able Sentry, Skopji, Macedonia			
	7/1st Avn Regt	3	UH-60A

Note: Maritime patrol aircraft (MPA) are tasked for short deployment (usually two weeks) in support of Operation Sharp Guard, the NATO/WEU embargo enforcement operation aimed at the former Yugoslavia. US and Canadian MPA are on longer deployments.

A 37th Airlift Squadron (AS) Lockheed Martin C-130E Hercules at Sarajevo airport in November 1994, showing off the then new 'gunship' grey paint scheme. To the right of the nose it is just possible to see the crater in the unloading area caused by a Bosnian Army 120mm mortar round two months earlier. UN soldiers were confident this was not a stray round! *(Tim Ripley)*

APPENDIX D
NATO/UN AIR LOSSES 1992–95

3.9.92. Alenia G.222. 48 Brigata, *Aeronautica Militare Italiana.* Shot down by heat-seeking SAM 17 miles west of Sarajevo. 4 crew killed.

26.3.93. Northrop Grumman E-2C Hawkeye. VAW-124, USS *Theodore Roosevelt*, USN. Non-combat loss in Adriatic. 5 crew killed.

12.4.93. Dassault Mirage 2000C. 5e EC, French *Armée de l'Air.* Non-combat loss during air-to-air refuelling over Adriatic. Pilot rescued.

11.8.93. Lockheed Martin F-16C. 23rd FS, USAF Non-combat loss over Adriatic, due to mechanical failure. Pilot rescued.

12.2.94. Grumman F-14 Tomcat F-14B, VF-103, USS *Saratoga*, USN. Non-combat loss over Adriatic after mid-air collision with McDonnell Douglas F/A-18C Hornet, also from USS *Saratoga*. Crew rescued. Hornet diverted safely to Italy.

16.2.94. Lockheed Martin F-16C. 526th FS, USAF. Non-combat loss at Portoroz, Slovenia, due engine failure. Pilot rescued.

16.4.94. Sea Harrier FRS.1. 801 Sqn, HMS *Ark Royal*, British Royal Navy. Shot down by Bosnian Serb heat-seeking SAM over Gorazde. Pilot rescued.

24.4.94. McDonnell Douglas F/A-18C. VFA-83, USS *Saratoga*, USN. Non-combat loss over Adriatic. Pilot killed.

15.12.94. Sea Harrier FRS.1, 800 Squadron, HMS *Invincible*, British Royal Navy. Non-combat loss over Adriatic. Pilot rescued.

1.1.95. Ilyushin Il-76, Bel-Air charter operator. Non-combat loss at Sarajevo airport during landing in high wind. Crew rescued.

26.1.95. Lockheed Martin F-16C Fighting Falcon. 510th FS, USAF. Non-combat loss over Adriatic. Pilot killed.

2.6.95. Lockheed Martin F-16C. 512th FS, USAF. Shot down by Bosnian Serb SA-6 SAM over western Bosnia. Pilot rescued after six days in Serb territory.

21.6.95. SEPECAT Jaguar GR.1. 54 Squadron, British RAF. Non-combat loss over Adriatic due to engine failure. Pilot rescued.

14.8.95. Westland Lynx AH.MK.7. 3 Regiment, Army Air Corps, British Army. Non-combat loss over Adriatic. Four killed and one crew rescued.

30.9.95. Dassault Mirage 2000K-2. 2/3e EC, French *Armée de l'Air.* Shot down by Bosnian Serb heat-seeking SAM over Pale. Crew captured but released on 20.12.95.

29.8.95. Lockheed Martin U-2R. 9th RW, USAF, Non-combat loss at RAF Fairford, UK. Pilot killed.

1.12.95. Aérospatiale SA 342 Gazelle, Det ALAT, non-combat loss in Croatia. Crew rescued.

APPENDIX E
OPERATION DELIBERATE FORCE: ORDNANCE EXPENDITURE

Type	Number Expended	Employing Aircraft
Precision Munitions		
LASER GUIDED BOMBS		
GBU-10 (2,000lb)	303	F-16C, F-15E, F/A-18C/D/EF-18A+
GBU-12 (500lb)	125	F-16C, F-15E, F/A-18/C/D/EF-18A+Jaguar (FR)
GBU-16 (1,000lb)	215	F/A-18C,EF-18A+/Harrier GR.7/Jaguar(FR)
GBU-24 (2,000lb)	6	F/A-18C/F-14
(penetrating warhead)		
AS-30L	4	Mirage 2000
ELECTRO-OPTICAL/INFRA-RED GUIDED MISSILE		
AGM-84 SLAM	10	F/A-18C
GBU-15 (2,000lb)	9	F-15E
AGM-63 Maverick	23	A-10A/F/A-18C
Tomahawk Land Attack Missiles	13	USS *Normandy*
Non-Precision Munitions		
BOMBS		
Mk 82 (500lb)	175	F-16A/A-10A/various
Mk 83 (1,000lb)	99	F-16A/Sea Harrier/various
Mk 84 (2,000lb)	42	F-16A/various
CBU-87 cluster bombs	2	
OTHER MUNITIONS		
30mm cannon	10,086	A-10A
40mm cannon	50	AC-130H
105mm cannon	350	AC-130H
2.75in rockets	20	A-10A
AGM-88 HARM	56	EA-6B/F-16C/FA-18A+/C/D

GLOSSARY

AAC: Army Air Corps (British Army)
ABCCC: Airborne Battlefield Command and Control Centre
ABiH/Armija: Army of Bosnia and Herzegovina (Muslim)
ACCS: Airborne Command and Control Squadron (USAF)
Aeronautica Militare Italiana: Italian Air Force
Aéronautique Navale: French Naval Aviation
AG: Air Group (USAF/ANG)
AG:Aufklanrungsgeschwader (German Air Force wing-sized reconnaissance unit)
ALAT: *Aviation Légère del'Armée de Terre* (French Army Aviation)
AOC: Air Operations Cell (UNHCR)
AOCC: Air Operations Control Centre
Armée de l'Air: French Air Force
ARS: Air Refuelling Squadron (USAF)
Aviazone per la Marine Militare (Italian Navy Aviation)
Avn: Aviation (US Army)
AW: Airlift Wing (USAF)
AWACS: Airborne Warning and Control System
BH: Bosnia–Herzegovina (UN/NATO term)
BiH: Republic of Bosnia–Herzegovina (Muslim)
BHC: Bosnia–Herzegovina Command (UN) (Became UNPROFOR 1 April 1995)
Bn: Battalion
BSA: Bosnian Serb Army
CAOC: Combined Air Operations Centre (NATO)
CAS: Close air support
CSAR: Combat search and rescue
Det: Detachment
EB: Escadre de Bombardment (French Air Force wing-sized strategic bomber/recce unit)
EC: Escadre de Chasse (French Air Force wing-sized fighter/bomber unit)
ECMM: European Community Monitoring Mission
ECS: Electronic Combat Squadron (USAF)
EDA: Escadre de Detection Aéroportée (French Air Force AWACS unit)
EET: Escadron Electronique Tactique (French Air Force electronic warfare squadron)
EE: Escadron Electronique (French Air Force electronic warfare squadron)
EH: Escadron d'helicopters (French Air Force helicopter squadron with CSAR role)
Ejercito del Aire: Spanish Air Force
ELINT: Electronic intelligence
ERV: Escadre de Ravitaillement (French Air Force tanker unit)
Escadron: French squadron sized unit
ET: Escadre de Transport (French Air Force wing-sized transport unit)
EU: European Union
5 ATAF: 5th Allied Tactical Air Force (NATO)
Flt: Flight
FG: Fighter Group (USAF)
Force Aerienne Belge: Belgian Air Force
FS: Fighter Squadron (USAF)
FRY: Former Republic of Yugoslavia
FW: Fighter Wing (USAF)
GBU: Guided bomb unit
HARM: High Speed Anti-Radiation Missile
HC: US Navy Helicopter Combat Support Squadron
HMLA: US Marine Helicopter Attack Squadron, Light
HMH: US Marine Helicopter Squadron, Heavy
HMM: US Marine Helicopter Squadron, Medium

HS: US Navy Helicopter Antisubmarine Squadron
HV: Hrvatska Vojska (Croatian Army)
HVO: Hrvatsko Vijece Odbrane (Croatian Defence Council, Croat militia in Bosnia)
IADS: Integrated air defence system
IFOR: Implementation Force (NATO)
JAOC: Joint Air Operations Cell (UNHCR)
JAP: Joint Action Plan (US diplomatic plan)
JBG: Jagdbombergeschwader (German Air Force wing-sized bomber unit)
JNA: Jugoslovenska Narodna Armija (Federal Yugoslav armed forces)
Luftwaffe: German Air Force
LTG: Lufttransportgeschwader (German Air Force wing-sized transport unit)
Marineflieger: German Naval Aviation
Maybe Airlines: UNHCR/UNPROFOR airbridge to Sarajevo
MFG: Marinefliegergeschwader (German Navy wing-sized unit)
MRE: Meals Ready to Eat (US military rations)
NAEWF: NATO Airborne Early Warning Force
NATO: North Atlantic Treaty Organisation
PRU: Photographic Reconnaissance Unit (RAF)
Regt: Regiment
RHC: Regiment d'Helicopters de Combat (French Army Aviation)
RHCM:Regiment d'Helicopters de Commandement et de Manoeuvre (French Army Aviation)
RRF: Rapid Reaction Force (UN)
RW: Reconnaissance Wing (USAF)
SAM: Surface-to-air missile
SHF: Support Helicopter Force (SHF)
SEAD: Suppression of enemy air defence
SLAM: Stand-off land attack missile
SOS: Special Operations Squadron (SOS)
Sqn: Squadron
Stormo: Italian Air Force wing-sized unit
TACP: Tactical air control party
TDY: Temporary duty (US military term)
TRIAD: Tri-Wall Aerial Distribution System
Turk Hava Kuvvetleri: Turkish Air Force
UN: United Nations
UNCRO: United Nations Confidence Restoring Operation(succeeded UNPROFOR in Croatia on 1/4/95)
UNHCR: United Nations High Commissioner for Refugees
UNMO: United Nations Military Observer
UNPF: United Nations Peace Forces (succeeded UNPROFOR on 1 April 1995)
UNPROFOR: United Nations Protection Force
USAF: United States Air Force
USS: United States Ship
VA: US Navy Attack Squadron
VAQ: US Navy Tactical Electronic Warfare Squadron
VAW: US Navy Carrier Airborne Early Warning Squadron
VF: US Navy Fighter Squadron
VFA: US Navy Strike Fighter Squadron
VMAQ: US Marine Tactical Electronic Warfare Squadron
VFMA(AW): US Marine All-Weather Fighter Attack Squadron
VFMA: US Marine Fighter Attack Squadron
VFA: US Navy Strike Fighter Squadron
VP: US Navy Patrol Squadron
VS: US Navy Antisubmarine Squadron
VQ: US Navy Fleet Reconnaissance Squadron
WEU: Western European Union
Wing: Air force units containing one or more squadrons.